Living Uncommonly

LIFE-CHANGING BIBLICAL PRACTICES
FOR LIVING A LIFE OF PURPOSE

Mark Harner

Ron —

I've enjoyed getting to know you and admire your deep relationship with Christ! I hope you find this book meaningful and helpful.

Mark

Caliente Press

ISBN: 978-1-943702-32-9 (print edition)
        978-1-943702-29-9 (Kindle edition)

Scripture quotations taken from The Holy Bible, New International Version® NIV®
Copyright © 1973 1978 1984 2011 by Biblica, Inc.™
Used by permission. All rights reserved worldwide.

Published by:
Caliente Press
1775 E Palm Canyon Drive, #110-198
Palm Springs, CA 92264
www.calientepress.com

Cover Design: Tri Widyatmaka

Endorsements

Living Uncommonly is for the common man who wants to live an uncommon life of passion and purpose. My friend, Mark Harner, took that challenge over forty-three years ago and it changed the course of his life and eternity. I believe as you read this book it will change your life as well.

> Kerry Shook
> Founding Pastor of Woodlands Church
> Co-author of the New York Times bestseller *One Month to Live*

Mark Harner has penned a wonderful and practical book that can serve as a useful guide to everyone from the new believer to the more mature Christian in how God desires us to live our lives with purpose. Anyone who truly desires to live and finish their life strong and in a way that is pleasing to God would do well to follow Mark's examples and the wisdom he shares with us in this book.

> Larry O'Donnell
> Former President
> Waste Management
> First Undercover Boss on the CBS Reality TV Series

Mark Harner brings his Christian faith to all areas of his life. His book presents his personal journey with Jesus Christ and his dependence upon the Bible as he seeks to live a purposeful life. His focus on his personal experiences as they relate to specific pieces of Scripture provides a very effective, thoughtful, and humble approach to his writing.

> Timothy R. Thyreen
> Chancellor
> Waynesburg University

Living Uncommonly is a roadmap for a life of faithful existence. Witnessing the author's Christian commitment and growth over four decades has been a privilege and reading his story is a joy.

Fred Depalma
Senior Vice President
Merrill Lynch Wealth Management

The Christian walk can often be an encounter between faith and the secular world. This book is a wonderful collection of life experiences filled with insightful perspectives on how to live, in this modern age, a life that witnesses to the grace and truth of Jesus Christ.

Doug Lee
President
Waynesburg University

I have known and admired Mark for most of his career with Waste Management and know him to be a man of character and a recognized and successful leader of a very critical part of our Fortune 200 company. This book is fantastic and right on point with superb insight from an experienced and committed husband, father, friend, mentor, and most importantly, Christ seeker. He brings a layman's view of the primary challenges every person should face and provides honest, real-life, practical methods to overcome those challenges, and all with a Biblical basis. It is delivered with humility, candor, truth, and practical personal insights that all together add up to useful everyday wisdom for everyone.

Jim Trevathan
Former Chief Operating Officer
Waste Management

When it comes to authentic Christian living, Mark Harner gets it! I have observed for nearly thirty years how he truly believes and lives the principles in this book. Read his faith story and life lessons in *Living Uncommonly* and you will be greatly encouraged to follow Jesus with your whole heart.

Dr. David Smith
Senior Pastor
Tusculum Baptist Church
Greeneville, TN

It's essential reading for everyone trying to navigate the right road though faith, family, business, and the Christian walk. Mark asks powerful questions which we all would be wise to consider.

Jason Jennaro
CEO
Breakwater Energy Partners

Mark reminds us that the Christian walk is a balance between "doing" and "being." In an action-oriented culture, our testimony, as demonstrated by our actions, must emanate from a relationship that motivates us and changes our very nature. And this becomes our legacy. We have to live intentional lives that rise above our circumstances. Living an outward-focused life requires an inner strength grounded in the principles Christ taught. Mark lays out in plain language these principles for people who are called to be anything but "plain."

Don Carpenter
Assistant Clinical Professor
Accounting and Business Law
Baylor University, Waco, TX

Mark has definitely found a new calling. His writing is effortless to read with a style I find very engaging. The principles Mark discusses in this book ring true to the man I first met when coaching him as a college athlete, then observed in him as a Corporate Executive and community leader. What began as a legacy for his grandchildren, and he is now graciously sharing with us in this book, truly represents his life of faith, integrity, and character. Mark illustrates pivotal life principles through his story. This book will challenge you to deepen your faith, to examine your core values, and clarify your life objectives.

Lowrie McCown
Head of School
Springwood School
Lannet, AL

Mark Harner has written an important book for any person, Christian or not, to read now and as they go through life. His insight, guided by his faith, will serve any reader who wishes to live life in its fullest. I personally wish I had this years ago. Thanks Mark, and thank the Holy Spirit for inspiring Mark!

Bob Simpson
Former Chief Financial Officer
Waste Management

Virtually everyone desires a fulfilling and significant life without settling for a simple common existence. In his book *Living Uncommonly*, Mark Harner reveals a proven plan, based on his own rich experiences, which leads to a life focused on fulfilling the purpose God has designed personally for you. An inspirational read for Christians and non-Christians alike, this book has insights that when applied will change your life.

Steve Fowler
CEO
Steve Fowler Consulting Inc.

Contents

Dedications

<u>To Cindy</u> — My wife of 39 years, love of my life and matriarch of our family, who greatly encouraged me as I wrote this book.

<u>To our four children</u> — Josh, Jenna, Jaymie, and Joanna, and sons-in-law Casey, Dustin, and Phil. I hope you find this book helpful in your own pursuit of Christ and as you parent your own children.

<u>To our five grandchildren</u> — Levi, Trace, Hayden, Trenton, and Mayleigh. You were the catalyst behind me writing this book. My goal is to positively impact your lives for many years to come and I hope that this book will provide some encouragement to you to passionately pursue Christ long after I am with the Lord in heaven.

<u>To my future descendants</u> — My prayer is that this book will help you come to know Christ in a personal and intimate way and that you will impact your sphere of influence in a substantial way for the sake of Christ. I look forward to meeting and loving you one day in heaven.

INTRODUCTION

You may be wondering why a non-celebrity like myself would write this book. What qualifies me to write a book that someone other than a family member might want to read (and maybe not even them!)?

Until recently, the thought of writing a book never crossed my mind. But then, it just became clear to me that it was something I needed to do — you might say a nudging by the Holy Spirit on my life. I also realized that this nudging by the Spirit may be because I have had many one-on-one experiences with non-believing men and have spent considerable time discipling men who believe. And, having been discipled myself over a number of years, these God-ordained experiences have given me insights into life that I believe are worth sharing.

From a personal perspective, I reasoned that if only my wife, four grown children, five grandchildren, and future great-grandchildren read this book, the effort of writing and editing it would be worth it. I want to leave a legacy for the young people in my family I may never meet, but for whom I already care about deeply.

As I write this introduction, I am 62 years old. My eldest grandchild is just four years old. My children, and certainly my wife, know my heart, but I don't know if my grandchildren (and future descendants) will ever fully know my thoughts on how they might live an effective and purposeful life. I'd like them to know my thinking so that they can incorporate that into their own personal reflections on how they want to live their lives. So this was my original purpose for writing and sharing my thoughts and creating this book.

However, after a handful of family members and friends read my initial drafts, the feedback was that the advice and experiences I was sharing would benefit a wider audience than just future generations of my own lineage. And as I listened to their comments and expanded my thinking, my hope now is that this book of practical advice based on Scripture will enable you each to find new ways to live lives of purpose. My aim is to help you develop practices that will draw you into a more intimate relationship with Christ and impact those in your sphere of influence in a substantially positive way.

There are a lot of Christ-followers who are doing things that are not going to make the headlines or cable news, but the things these everyday followers of Christ are doing are significant to their families and simultaneously are critical to the greater body of Christ and society. Even more important, the things these committed followers are doing are increasing their individual intimacy level with Christ. At the end of the day, I would argue that there is nothing more important in life than for each individual person to develop a deep, personal relationship with Jesus Christ. This book aims to help you on that journey.

Conversely, there are a lot of Christians who do not seem to understand their life's real purpose, or who are not focused on truly placing Christ first in their lives. If we let it, the cares of this life will engulf us or, at a minimum, take our focus off what Christ would have for us. I have been meeting regularly with an atheist for five plus years discussing the big questions of life. He has not yet crossed the line of faith, but he has told me one thing that should give pause to every believer about the state of Christianity (at least in America). He said that, based on his own personal observations, only a very small percentage of Christians are truly trying to live a purposeful life for Christ. He meets with me only because he sees me in that small percentage (rightly or wrongly). I hope the personal experiences I share with you like this in *Living Uncommonly* resonate with you and help you as you consider how you might make Christ Lord of every area of your life.

I believe that the topics in this book are important matters for every believer, and non-believer alike, to consider as each of us searches for meaning, significance, and greater purpose in this life. Some believers reading this book may feel distant or stagnant in their relationship with Christ. Others may be new in your faith and are seeking to learn more about how to live your new-found faith. Or, you may be a person considering the claims of Christ who wants an additional perspective as you investigate the Christian faith. I have been in every one of those stages of life, and more. So, no matter where you are in life, know that I am not much different than you. And most likely, most of you will be just like me, a person who will never make the headlines but who will have the opportunity to make a significant, positive difference in the lives of others.

If you are a person considering Christianity, I encourage you to keep reading this book. I hope that the topics that I write about will pique your interest in the person of Jesus Christ. In addition, many of the things I write about are just plain good for every person. You may not know it now, but what Jesus Christ says in the Bible about such topics as relationships, money, and priorities, if followed, could help you avoid trouble in life. They may also help you focus more so that you are more effective in everything you do in your life.

This book is organized in short chapters on topics that every person deals with, or should deal with, and for which I have had personal experiences. I am certainly not the expert on each of these topics, but hopefully my thoughts will be helpful in your life and provide some "take-aways" that you can use on a daily basis. Each chapter can be read independently and do not need to be read in the order they appear in the book, except for the first chapter *(My Personal Spiritual Journey – Crossing the Line of Faith)* and the last chapter (*Finishing Strong*).

Also, each chapter has a keynote Scripture reference right under the title of the chapter. These Scriptures form the core foundation for my thoughts on each topic. All of these references are from the New International Version (NIV) Bible.

I will start this book with a discussion of how I entered into a personal relationship with Jesus Christ 43 years ago and how this changed the course of my life forever. I will also give you a little background on me, so you have a frame of reference when I write on the various topics. Thank you in advance for joining me on this journey.

Mark Harner
Spring, Texas
September 2019

CHAPTER 1

My Personal Spiritual Journey. Crossing the Line of Faith.

I (Jesus Christ) tell you the truth,
whoever hears My word and believes Him who sent Me
has eternal life and will not be condemned;
*he has **crossed over from death to life**.*
John 5:24

I was born in Gettysburg, PA in 1957, so you might say I have a little history in my blood. My parents, Robert and Juanita Harner, who are both deceased, raised me and my older brother Jeff in a loving home. One of the things I learned from my parents, and to this day I try to emulate with my own children and grandchildren, is that I always felt like my well-being was more important than their own. I don't know if that was really true, but they definitely made me feel that way, which provided a sense of security and self-worth. I want my children and grandchildren to feel the same from me.

My Mom and Dad were married at ages 19 and 21, respectively, and remained married for 53 years until my Mom's death from cancer in 2006. My Dad passed away from a number of health complications in 2013. My Dad worked for American Water Works his entire 44-year career before retiring at age 62. He was a high school graduate who eventually ascended to be a President of a subsidiary within this multi-billion-dollar organization. He was an achiever, and I suppose that inspired me to be one as well.

My Mom was a homemaker her entire life, a job that, in my opinion, is usually harder and more complex than that of the major breadwinner of the family. My Mom was good at it. She also supported my Dad well and loved to attend various business events with him. My Dad had a close circle of friends around his work and the spouses of these friends were some of my Mom's best friends.

My brother Jeff is two years older than me. He was a medical doctor his entire career, specializing in radiology until his retirement a few years ago. His wife, Heather, is currently a practicing attorney and they live in York, PA. They have two grown children and one grandchild. From the earliest time that I can remember, even as a young child, my brother always expressed that he wanted to be a doctor, which he accomplished. Jeff is also an accomplished pianist, though he has never played professionally. Although we are close in age, Jeff and I never competed against each other since we had different interests (mine were primarily sports). That was good in that we did not have any sibling envy, but bad in that we did not spend as much time together as most brothers only two years apart in age would normally do.

As for myself, I received a Business degree in 1979 from Waynesburg University in Waynesburg, PA, majoring in Accounting and received my Certified Public Accountant (CPA) license in 1980. About ten years later, I got my Masters of Business Administration (MBA) from Old Dominion University in Norfolk, VA, when I was working for Newport News Shipbuilding in various financial management roles during an 11-year period.

I began my working career in Pittsburgh, PA with Deloitte, at the time one of the "Big Eight" accounting firms. I finished my career in Houston, TX, where I currently live, working for Tenneco, and then for Waste Management as a Vice President for 14 years, building and running all their back-office administrative operations in both Houston and Phoenix.

My wife, Cindy, and I married in 1980. We were high school sweethearts, you might say, as we met during our junior year in high school and dated exclusively until our marriage. Cindy received her Associates Degree in Business from a local Community College and, except for the first year of our marriage, has been a Homemaker. We have four grown children, three daughters who are married, a son who is single, along with five grandchildren.

Now that you know a little bit about my family, I'll return to the beginning of my story. My Dad was promoted several times in his career and this required our family to move fairly frequently. We left Gettysburg when I was four years old for Peoria, IL, then Kokomo, IN, when I was seven. It was there that my love for sports, particularly basketball, started. This would later be a significant part of the story of my spiritual transformation. We then moved to Greensburg, PA, near Pittsburgh, when I was 12. I consider Pittsburgh home, as I spent my significant growing-up years there and did not leave until I was 27 years old. My wife was born and raised in the Pittsburgh area, and her four siblings all still live there. By the way, Pittsburgh also has a very good football team — my beloved Pittsburgh Steelers!

My parents were church attenders and took my brother and me to church every Sunday. I was confirmed in a Protestant church as an early teen. I saw church as an important activity in my life, though not necessarily as my highest priority. I definitely believed in God, but really did not understand what it meant to have a personal relationship with Jesus Christ.

As I just mentioned, sports became a high priority in my life. I was a starter on the football and basketball teams at the large high school that Cindy and I attended, and I was All-Conference in both sports as a senior. I was also the starting shortstop on the baseball team my senior year. That was back in the days when you could play all sports and not have to specialize in one sport, as many young people do today. Cindy was a cheerleader, so you get the picture — local high school jock dates cheerleader. There is no doubt that much of my self-worth was tied to athletics. It also fueled the idea that if you worked hard and had a measure of talent, success should be the result. I suppose that this also made it harder for me to later accept the idea of God's free grace toward me through Jesus Christ.

I was recruited to play football in college by several schools, but I determined that I was never going to do that, because of the physical demands of the sport, unless I got a full scholarship, which I didn't. My first love was basketball anyway, so when I received a partial scholarship to play basketball at a small school, about 75 minutes from my home (Waynesburg University), I was anxious to go. I went off to school, hoping to do well in school and basketball and get a good job; basic goals for a college kid. While I wanted to do well at basketball, I knew that college basketball would be the end of the line for me as far as organized sports.

For the most part, school was fine and basketball okay (I never did garner significant playing time in college, though I did play all four years). I was probably not unlike most college first-year students, not being very sure of myself in a new environment. I lived in a dormitory and a man by the name of Mark Bianchi was the dorm director. He also happened to be the assistant basketball coach. I saw in Mark something that I didn't have. He seemed to have a real sense of peace and true purpose about him, something I definitely lacked at the time.

I soon learned that Mark called himself a Christian and that it was the most important thing in his life. That was curious to me, as I called myself a Christian too (if someone would ask me), but I knew I was not a Christian like Mark was, and I certainly would not say that faith was the most important thing in my life.

After getting to know Mark better over the first few months of school and spending regular time talking with him in his dorm suite, he asked me a question one night which put me back on my heels. He said, "Mark, if you were to die today, would you be certain that you would go to heaven?"

My initial reaction was one of indignation — what gave him the right to ask me such a question? Besides, how does anyone answer such a question? After stammering a bit, I told Mark that I did not believe anyone could know the answer to that question with certainty, but based upon the fact that I was a "good guy," I thought there was a good probability that I would go to heaven.

I believed in the "good guy" theory of salvation. I had never committed any of the big sins — drugs, murder, stealing, etc. I did not drink much. I did not even swear much. From the view of most people, I probably was a good guy. But I was not at peace about being able to answer this question like Mark was.

Along the way, Mark quoted a Scripture to me from 1 John 5:11-13 that says:

> *"And this is the testimony, God has given us eternal life, and this life is in His Son. He who has the Son has life. He who does not have the Son of God does not have life. I write these things to you who believe in the name of the Son of God so that you may know that you have eternal life."*

I did not reject the Bible as truth. I generally believed in it, but I am sure I thought there were some loopholes in it. Still, these verses kind of "cut to the chase." They bothered me in the sense that I did not have the certainty that these verses communicated. Still, I was not ready to take any action at that point, or to fully embrace 1 John 5:11-13 as truth.

Mark continued to talk to me about the Bible and the person of Jesus Christ over the next few months. Then, one day he invited me to a weekend conference called *Jubilee*, which would be attended by some 2000 college students in downtown Pittsburgh (about 50 miles from my campus). I agreed to attend with him, along with probably another 20-30 students from Waynesburg.

On Sunday, February 29, 1976, the keynote speaker was a man by the name of Tom Skinner, a former New York City black gang leader who had become a Christian. At the end of his message, he invited all in the crowd who wanted to be able to answer positively and without doubt the question that Mark had asked me weeks earlier to stand and enter into a relationship with Jesus Christ. He said if you wanted your sins forgiven and to be reconciled back to God, and to know for certain that you would go to heaven when you died, to stand up and pray a short prayer along with him to accept Jesus Christ as your personal Savior and Lord. It was my spiritual moment of truth. I did not really want to stand and do this, but I wanted to be forgiven and to have the question definitively answered. So, I stood and prayed to receive Christ as Savior and Lord. As John 5:24 says, at that moment, I **"crossed over from death to life."**

What I did not fully understand then, but certainly do now, is that I was a terrible sinner in desperate need of a Savior. I may have been a "good guy" in the eyes of many people, but in relation to God, I fell far short of His perfect standard. I was focused on myself, not on God. I now realize that even if I only ever committed one sin in my life (which, of course, isn't close to being accurate), I was still in a situation where I was separated from God. He is perfect and I am not. There is no reason for a perfect God to have imperfect people live with Him in eternity, except for His divine grace toward man. But just like every person who has ever lived, I had already committed sin. I needed something to account for that sin, and Jesus Christ came to do just that for you and for me. He came so that every person could have an opportunity to be reconciled back to God.

It does not matter the "level" of sin a person has committed. The cold, hard facts are that every person has sinned, and every person is a sinner, apart from Jesus Christ. You may be or have been like me, a basically good person in the eyes of our fellow human beings. Or you may have been someone who deeply wronged someone close to you, committed a horrific crime, or done some other thing that seems just unforgivable. That does not matter in the eyes of Christ.

Every one of us is a sinner in desperate need of a Savior. No matter the level of sin in the eyes of man, every single one of those sins needs to be forgiven by Christ's shed blood on the cross. And the good news is, when a person <u>receives</u> Christ as personal Savior and Lord, that person is forgiven and will live eternally with Christ in heaven. As the Bible states, ***"Yes to all who received Him, to those who believed in His name, He gave the right to become children of God" (John 1:12).***

Not only does He want to save us from our sin, but I soon learned that He wants us to live an abundant life while on earth. In John 10:10, Jesus says, ***"I have come that they might have life, and have it more abundantly."***

Following my spiritual transformation at *Jubilee,* I now had the capacity to have true meaning and purpose in life. I was now positioned to live an abundant life — a life where peace, purpose, contentment, and joy are more dominant than they ever were before. A life where I could now come to know Christ better and experience the blessings and challenges in life that only He can bring.

One side note before I end my story. One of the great things about receiving Christ as personal Savior is that you now enter into a brand-new family on this earth. A family that does not care what your race, gender, age, or financial status is. A family where it does not matter where you came from. You are now part of the greater body of Jesus Christ — the church. You have the strongest bond that you can have with any other person — the bond of faith in Jesus Christ.

Back to my story. So, you might ask — what changed? Frankly, I don't remember the changes to be that drastic. But my wife, who was then my girlfriend, remembers it a bit differently. She says I spoke much more about Jesus and that my priorities and world view were changing. I guess that was true as she came to faith in Christ about a year later. What I remember changing most were my priorities, which really changed my whole thought process. Life was no longer about just pleasing Mark Harner. Rather, it became about serving Christ and changing my priorities to put Him first in my life, as best I could.

I had the good fortune of being discipled the next three years by Lowrie McCown, who took over the assistant coaching duties a year later when Mark left. That formed the roots for my Christian faith moving forward. Since then, I have sought to be involved in solid Bible-believing, gospel-preaching churches, and have regularly sought out opportunities for growth and discipleship outside the church as well. In the chapter on *Disciple-Making*, I write about being discipled in my late 20s and 30s in Newport News, Virginia by a man by the name of Frank Satchell, which was also key to my spiritual development.

Additionally, I have developed a daily quiet time routine of prayer and Bible reading, something I will share with you in a later chapter. I am still a work in progress and will be like that until the day I die and Christ brings me into heaven. But hopefully, I will keep trying to grow in intimacy with Christ, which in my view is the most important activity any person can engage in while on this earth. I have also determined what my life purpose is (hint 1 Peter 3:15) for my remaining time on this earth; another thing I will share and write about in a later chapter.

Recently, I learned that the *Jubilee* conference celebrated its 40th anniversary a few years ago. Amazingly, I also found out that the very first Jubilee event was the one that I attended. I am forever grateful for Jesus Christ leading Mark to speak with me and invite me to that conference. It transformed my life forever. That transformation has led me to write about the topics included in this book.

CHAPTER 2

Living a Life of Purpose

*Now it is God who has made us for this very purpose
and has given us the Spirit as a deposit,
guaranteeing what is to come.*
2 Corinthians 5:5

As I write this book, I am now 62 years old. I am ashamed to say it, but not until the last few years have I really tried to define what my purpose is in life. Sure, I have known for most of my Christian life that I am to love the Lord with all my heart, soul, and mind, and that I am to love my neighbor as myself (Matthew 22:37-39). I have known that I am supposed to be salt and light (Matthew 5:13-16).

There are several verses like these in the Bible that are clear as to what our purpose in life is to be. Ultimately, we are to bring glory to God in everything that we do and say. Those are the broad purposes for every human being (whether we realize it or not).

We could live our lives under these broad purposes and probably lead a life that is pleasing to Christ and is generally impactful. But I think there is more to it than that. Have you ever really thought about your specific purpose(s) in life? Is there any paramount purpose that Jesus Christ has for you while you remain on this earth?

Most of us go through life not wanting to think about the purpose and strategy for our life. It requires deep thought, time alone, and certainly time in the Word and prayer. If you are like me, you would rather be a "doer" and just execute on whatever comes your way in life. Living a life of intention and specific purpose requires effort. Besides, what if we make a mistake in our efforts to get too specific?

The Pastors of the church I go to, Kerry and Chris Shook, wrote a New York Times bestseller about ten years ago entitled *One Month to Live*. In the book, they ask the question: "If you knew you only had one month to live, how would you spend that last month?"

Thinking about these questions tends to make us have a clearer focus in life. It helps us to focus on that which is truly important. As you try to hone in on the purpose God has for you in this life, you might want to think about it as if you only had 30 days to live. More importantly, how can you have that attitude throughout every day of your life, even though your life expectancy might be much longer?

Here is another way to think about it. If you are a believer, why has God kept you on this earth? The Christian is going to live eternally with Him. Why doesn't He just take us to heaven and stop the unnecessary and sometimes futile efforts we make at the various pursuits we have in our lives? I have often asked that question of myself. He must have me here for a reason. Otherwise, it does not make sense that any Christian is still here on this earth. It seems to me imperative that we find that foremost reason for our remaining existence on earth.

As you look for that purpose in your own life, keep in mind that it will almost always be related to relationships, and not material things. I am not saying that all material things are evil and that God does not use material resources in our lives to impact others for the glory of Jesus Christ. Of course, He does that. But I find it hard to believe that God will leave me here longer so that I can do things like build up my investment accounts, or take that "bucket list" trip, or achieve some award. But it does seem completely logical to me that He will leave me here on earth so that He can use me to reach another person for Christ.

Remember, God's "Plan A" for reaching people with the saving grace of Jesus Christ is to use other imperfect people to do so. And there is no "Plan B." God uses Christians, empowered by the Holy Spirit within them, to introduce non-Christians to Him.

Your prevailing purpose should be found at the intersection of your best abilities and your God-given passions. Below are a few steps you can take to help you define your overriding purpose:

- Note specific Scripture(s) which inspire a passion within you. Maybe it is a specific passage, or a series of Scriptures, but it is important that the purpose you identify is based on Scripture.

- Take note of ministries that you are attracted to.

- Make sure you understand what your spiritual gift(s) are, and how you might one day use them as you define your purpose (see a list of these gifts in Romans 12:4-8; 1 Corinthians 12:7-11; Ephesians 4:11-13).

- Speak to other committed Christians who know you well and that you trust. Ask for their feedback on where they see you to be particularly effective.

All of this must be contemplated in prayer. There is probably no more important activity for us to engage in than to find our purpose and to seek an answer to that question through prayer. I guarantee that if you ask God to help you find your predominant purpose in life, He will answer that prayer. It is a prayer squarely in the center of His will for your life.

I believe that my primary spiritual gifts are encouragement and evangelism. I have come to this conclusion based on my own personal research using the four bullet points above. I know these two areas are where my passion resides. I meet with several men on a regular basis; some in discipleship relationships and some in evangelistic relationships. There is no doubt that evangelistic relationships inspire me more and interest me more. It is where my deepest passion is. As a result, in searching the Scriptures, I have determined that my primary life purpose is described very accurately in 1 Peter 3:15:

> *"But in your hearts set apart Christ as Lord. Always be prepared to give an answer to everyone who asks you to give the reason for the hope that you have. But do this with gentleness and respect."*

As I mentioned at the beginning of this chapter, I have recently come to this revelation about my purpose — in about the last three years. I have probably known it for about five years, but never ascribed a Scripture to it. Let me share with you an example of how this Scripture affected my actions on one particular day in the last year.

I was scheduled to meet one of the men that I have a regular evangelistic relationship with one day. I was to meet the man in downtown Houston at his lunch hour. I had nothing on my calendar for that day except that one meeting. My trip down to Houston would take about an hour and I would be able to meet with him for about an hour. So, I would need to take about three hours out of my day, in the middle of the day, to meet with him. Because this was the middle of the day, I would not be able to do much else that day (like play golf!).

I thought seriously about rescheduling that meeting. I mean, I could have a completely free day, which was and still is a rarity in my daily schedule. I even mentioned my intentions to cancel the meeting to my wife. But then it came to me that my life purpose was really all about what Scripture says in 1 Peter 3:15. Indeed, my job was to meet with this man. If I did not, I would be missing out on the purpose for which God was keeping me on this earth. I had a responsibility to be obedient to Him in what He had called me to do.

A funny thing about that day. The man I was supposed to meet with forgot about our meeting. So, I went all the way to downtown Houston and waited for about half an hour until it became apparent that he was not going to show. My first thought was, "What a waste of time!" But I quickly realized that such thinking was coming from my human tendencies, and not from the Spirit of Christ living in me. Regardless of the outcome, I had been obedient to Christ that day. I had acted on the purpose He had given me. The Christian does not do things based solely on results, as most non-Christians do. We do things based on obedience to that for which we have been called.

First Peter 3:15 came specifically to my mind that day as I considered what I would do — keep my meeting or cancel it. When I remembered what my purpose in life is, at least my principal purpose, my course of action became clear. There was no need to question it or doubt it. Knowing my purpose made my decision for that day easy to make. And knowing my purpose made it easy not to get frustrated when I achieved no "results" that day.

Three points of caution here. I firmly believe it is essential to research and find the prevailing purpose that God has given us in this earthly life. However, sometimes we can take it further than we should when we execute our purpose to the exclusion of our family. How many times, for instance, have we seen a Pastor lose his family because He had "God's work" to do at the church? We must always take our purpose seriously, but we must always maintain a balance that is healthy and God-honoring.

Secondly, there are times in our lives when we may need to fill a gap of service, even if it is outside our purpose. For instance, maybe you need to volunteer in the children's area of your church for a season, even though you know that is not within your primary purpose. Allow some flexibility here. Do not be so self-righteous about your purpose that you cannot display some humility and meet the need that might be before you.

Finally, recognize that your overriding purpose may shift some as you enter a new season of life. What God has called you to today may change a year, five years, or ten years from now. But before you recognize this fully, subject the change to the tests described in the four bullet points above. Your goal is to be as effective as you can be for the sake of God's kingdom on this earth. Make sure any change you make in your paramount purpose is from Him and not based on your own human desire.

CHAPTER 3

Making the Most of Every Opportunity

Be very careful then, how you live —
not as unwise but as wise,
making the most of every opportunity,
because the days are evil.
Ephesians 5:15-16

Six years ago, I gave a eulogy at my father's funeral. I spoke about the "Six Things I Learned from my Dad." Though my father was not my "spiritual father," he taught me an important principle which I was later to learn was also an important Biblical principle — Make the Most of Every Opportunity. That principle is clearly stated above in the keynote verse for this chapter (Ephesians 5:15-16). It is repeated in Colossians 4:5, this time referring to the way a Christian is to act toward a person who does not know Jesus Christ as their Savior and Lord.

As I just alluded to, making the most of every opportunity is not just a spiritual principle. It is inherent in the areas of business, sports, and politics, just to name a few. Most people want to maximize their experiences in life. We are taught that the way to get ahead is to develop strategies that will maximize our efforts to achieve the goals we set out for ourselves. At a company where I worked many years ago, I was once put on the strategy team to develop a comprehensive strategy for the business. I spent a full year dedicated to the development of this strategy. We produced a thick, fancy book, complete with many colorful graphs and impressive business insights. However, I am still not sure to this day how much of it was actually implemented.

Please understand that I have nothing against the development of strategies in business, sports, and politics; or even in the church. They can be useful and help us to increase focus in our jobs and our daily lives. In fact, this book contains a chapter on finding your life purpose in order to live a more effective and productive life. But what we must guard against is not seeing the opportunities that are right in front of us because we are solely focused on the bigger picture or future goals.

Think about it. How many times have you walked away from an encounter with another person where you later thought to yourself, "Why didn't I do that?" or "Why didn't I say this?" If the truth would be known, I sometimes go into an encounter with only an end result in mind, not thinking about the spiritual opportunity that God might be placing before me.

I am an agenda-driven guy. I also like to accomplish things and "check things off my list." I often try to fit more into my day than I can really accomplish. Can you other Type-A personalities relate to this? But there are great dangers in this.

First, this type of approach is most often a self-centered approach, and not aligned with what should be my desire to put Christ first above my own agenda. It can be a display of selfishness, of being a person who sits on the personal throne of their own life instead of allowing Christ to sit on their throne.

Second, and what this chapter is really all about, I might miss an opportunity Christ has placed in my life because I am too worried about accomplishing my agenda for the day, week, month, or year. My spiritual "antennae" is just not up when I am too focused on my personal to-do list.

Each of us has things that we must do every day. Many of you reading this book need to go to work every day. Or, you may be a stay at home Mom or Dad that needs to attend to young children every day. Most of us have inevitable priorities that dictate how we spend the balance of each day. But how many of us are on "red alert" to respond to God's unexpected priorities for us in each day?

Most of us, when we wake up in the morning, mentally go through our agendas for the day. We think about where we will spend our day and what we might accomplish. Even on the weekends, we still think about our activities — like golf, barbecuing, or maybe even shopping! But how many of us wake up every day and ask God to help us make the most of every opportunity for His glory that He might bring our way that day? If we did, we would be more likely to find God placing those opportunities in our paths because our priorities would be His priorities.

At the end of your life, you will care little about what you accomplished, say ten years prior, that had nothing to do with God's will for your life and/or the impact you had on others. But I think that you and I will care greatly about how we put Christ on the throne of our life and how that impacted the lives of others for eternity.

To live a life where we maximize opportunities, one of the things we need to defeat in our lives, with the help of Jesus Christ, is to be content with not accomplishing anything tangible for the day (at least as we define tangible in our own minds). At times, we may be an unknown link in the chain of God working in the life of another human being. If we are having a spiritual conversation with someone, we may not lead that person to faith in Christ, but we may say something that will cause them to believe in the future.

In fact, you may never know that until you get to heaven. Are you comfortable with not checking an item off your to-do list to take unexpected time to say a good word to someone else that God has placed in your path for that day? That is a question we must ask ourselves if we are going to be committed to making the most of every opportunity God places in our path.

Ephesians 5:15 tells us to "be very careful how we live" to make the most of every opportunity. In other words, if we are to make the most of every opportunity, we must be very intentional about our daily lives. If we do not have our minds and spirits focused every day on God's opportunities, we are likely going to miss them every time.

But how can we consistently do this day after day? It all begins with our daily Quiet Time of prayer and Bible study where we offer ourselves to God for the day. The apostle Paul makes a clear statement about this in Romans 12:1 – *"Therefore, I urge you, brothers, in view of God's mercy, to offer your bodies as living sacrifices, holy and pleasing to God – this is your spiritual act of worship."*

And it should continue every minute of every day as we maintain a dialogue with God throughout the day. As Paul describes in 1 Thessalonians 5:17, **"pray continually."** If we allow Scriptures like these to get our hearts and minds set on Him (Colossians 3:2), we can then go out in life day after day waiting and watching for Christ to bring us opportunities to positively affect the lives of others.

Ephesians 5:15 also tells us to be wise and not unwise. Not everything that comes our way unexpectedly is necessarily the God-orchestrated event that we are to engage in that day. We still must use discernment to know when we are to "plug-in" to another person's life. When we have our spiritual antennae up, there is also a danger to over-spiritualize every event in our lives. Pursuing intimacy with Christ in our daily quiet time, and maintaining that prayer dialogue throughout the day, will help us to be discerning of what God has truly placed in our lives.

Sometimes, it does not require a whole lot of discernment to determine when God is telling us to engage. Rather, it requires obedience and a willingness to go where God leads. In my second career, I am in real estate. About a year ago, I received a text from a former business associate who I had not seen in several years, but who I had known for nearly 20 years. He was looking for help in selling his home. But at the end of the text message, he made a very direct statement. He said, "My life is in a shambles."

Clearly, this was an opportunity that Christ was presenting to me that I should make the most of. However, I was already meeting one-on-one with a number of men on a regular basis. I wondered if I had the time and energy to add another. But the truth is, I did. Most of us will make time for those things that we deem truly important. If I truly valued the opportunity to point people to Christ, which I said I did, I needed to act on this. It was not a matter of discernment, but rather a matter of obedience.

Of course, not every opportunity will be this apparent. Some will indeed require a level of discernment that you may need to also discuss with your spouse, family, or close friends. But at least take the step to pray and consult with others, if you think necessary, when you believe the Lord might be leading you in a particular direction with a relationship.

There is another kind of opportunity that we should consider. It is those opportunities that you actively pursue because of a passion in an area God may have placed on your heart, and for which He has spiritually gifted you. It is not that you generate these opportunities on your own.

Rather, you engage in areas where you know God is at work and for which He has laid such a passion on your heart.

As an example, I volunteer to follow-up with those people at our church who mark on their attendance card that they are "Considering Christ." Evangelism is an area of passion for me and for which I believe He has gifted me. After our Easter services in 2017, I followed up with a man who had marked his card as "Considering Christ." He had some questions and doubts and was also a bit skeptical. I met with him regularly one-on-one for over a year as we examined a number of big questions that he had about Christianity. In the summer of 2018, he committed his life to Christ.

If I had not submitted to and pursued a known opportunity in an area of spiritual giftedness, I would have never had the privilege of helping to lead this man to Christ. It is important that you determine where your passion and gifts are and then pursue the opportunities that already exist in those areas.

There is a song by a Christian singer named Josh Wilson entitled *Dream Small*. The song is careful not to dismiss the idea of having big goals in your life. There is certainly a place for those, particularly as each of us determines our primary purposes in life, which I have encouraged you to do in the chapter on *Living a Life of Purpose*. But as previously mentioned, we must stay attuned to those everyday, seemingly small (at the time) opportunities that come our way. So, as you wake up and ask the Lord to use you for the glory of His Kingdom in the day that He has given you, be sure to "Dream Small." What you think is small today, may just become huge in someone's life later on.

As you can see from reading this chapter, making the most of every opportunity is a biblical concept aimed at how we impact the relationships we have with family, friends, and strangers. It may have application for other areas of life, but biblically, it is primarily aimed at relationships. There are only two things in this world that will last into eternity — the Word of God and the souls of people. Making the most of every opportunity is about impacting the souls of people that will last into eternity.

I encourage you not to miss out on this important spiritual principle in your life as you go through your daily activities. You will not only be obedient to and grow in your intimacy with Christ, but you may even impact the life of another person into eternity. Can there be anything more important than that?

CHAPTER 4

Making Your Work Spiritually Significant

Whatever you do, whether in word or deed,
do it all in the name of the Lord Jesus,
giving thanks to God the Father through Him.
Colossians 3:17

I have both experienced and observed something over the years about the way most people approach their jobs. It may not be true for everyone, but as a general rule, most people seem to go through a "life cycle" in their approach to work. The life cycle goes like this:

> 20s – Very focused on developing a career. Spend more hours at work, or working at home, than you probably should. If married, you begin to feel the tension of work/life balance; and even more so if you have children. But work seems to take precedence over most other things, and you justify it as you are just starting out and you need to "establish" yourself, provide for your family, and plant seeds for future success.

> 30s – Much of what I just wrote still applies, but now you may have a family and children's activities have

begun in earnest. But, at the same time, you have likely taken on more responsibility at work, so the work/life balance issue is now in full bloom. You find yourself constantly having to choose between work and family. In many ways, you feel guilty about not being able to give your work, or your family, your best. There is not a lot of time for anything else.

40s – The pressure to "do well" financially is now vital as college for your children will soon be upon you. This may cause you to continue to "grind it out" at work even harder. But at the same time, you begin to physically feel not quite like you did earlier in your life. So, you may need to get to the gym to stay healthier if you are going to be there for your children and spouse long-term. This adds another activity to an already full calendar. In addition, you may begin to feel the dreaded "mid-life crisis" coming at you, so you look to add excitement to your life, sometimes at great cost to you and your family.

50s – You now spend a lot of time thinking about retirement, looking to set yourself up for the next 20-30 years beyond age 65. As a result, you need to buckle down and try to maximize your earnings, as age 65 will be here before you know it. Besides, you have likely maxed out (or come close to maxing out) your career growth and increased earning potential. You begin to wonder if you should have done something else with your one and only life. Further, grandchildren may now be in the picture, adding another activity (though hopefully a good activity) that clutters up an already busy schedule. For some, this is a time when you are just "hanging on" trying to get to retirement so you can one day live "the good life."

60s – This will be another significant time of transition as you shift from working every day to retirement. In your early 60s you need to begin to plan what you will do in your later 60s. You want to do something meaningful but do not want to do something that takes up too much time. You will also want flexibility in your schedule, so you will have time to travel, see grandchildren, etc. You feel the pressure to make sure you have enough money and that your healthcare will be taken care of. Your financial planner becomes one of your better friends. Another transition may take place too — you and your spouse will now see a lot more of each other. Hopefully, that will be a good thing and not a bad thing! And finally, you may now feel like you have the time to volunteer in areas you have a passion for.

I will stop there because this chapter is not about post-retirement; it's about living through all the stages of life described above with greater purpose. It's about starting to live with a greater purpose from the time of reading this book forward. If you are a young person just starting out in the working world, please pay special attention to this chapter. You can live a life of greater meaning and purpose now, not just sometime in the future.

In the chapter on *Trusting Christ in Uncertain Times*, I wrote that at the end of your life, if you are a Christian, the thing that will be most important to you will be the level of development of your relationship to Christ. You will have wanted to place the priorities of Christ above your own. If you are not a Christian, keep reading anyway, as you may find some things that will help you; and start your pursuit of a relationship with Christ today!

Look again at the keynote verse of this chapter — Colossians 3:17, ***"Whatever you do, whether in word or deed, do it all in the name of the Lord Jesus, giving thanks to God the Father through Him."*** For the Christian, nothing (no word or deed) is to be done without Jesus Christ in mind. And, we are to have an attitude of gratitude about everything that we are engaged in or which comes our way. The verse says nothing about when we are to start doing that. The clear implication is that we are to do it <u>now</u>, no matter what stage of life you or I are in.

If you are a young person, I encourage you to take this concept to heart early on in your life. The sooner that you do, the sooner you will find meaning and purpose in everything that you do; and you will be much more effective for Christ in your daily activities. If you are an older person (like me!), it's not too late to start. Start right now!

So how do you put this into practice? First, it must start with a daily prayer of humility. Rather than rattle off your list of the areas where you need God's help in your life, start your daily prayer by submitting your life to Christ. Romans 12:1 tells us to offer our bodies as living sacrifices. Offer yourself daily to Christ in such a way. Ask Christ to open your eyes to what He is trying to tell you in your daily circumstances, including being very sensitive to the physical and spiritual needs of those around you. Ask Him for the sensitivity to see, and then the courage, margin, and willingness to sacrifice so that you can act on what He shows you.

When we are consumed by the demands of our personal lives with little to no margin, we often miss the people and opportunities that God places in our paths to impact others for Him. It is okay to rattle off your list of needs. He wants to hear that too. He just wants your priorities to be His priorities. If you will be consistent in earnestly doing this every day, I promise you that there is no way God will not answer that prayer, since you will have your heart right in the middle of His will.

I mentioned the word "margin" above. Even for those of us who really want to see Christ at work in everything that we do, oftentimes there just does not seem to be enough margin in our lives to get it done. Rather than always trying to "create margin," I suggest that you find margin right where you are in your job.

Lunchtime is a great time to follow-up with people that God may be nudging you to minister to. Last time I checked, most people need to eat. Invite the person that God is revealing to you to become involved with to lunch. Maybe it's breakfast or coffee. If you are married, talk it over with your spouse and invite the person to dinner at your home or out at a restaurant. It is okay to try to create margin, but do not overlook the margin already built into your life. You may simply need to use that built-in margin a little more creatively.

It's time for true confessions. I do not think I truly started "practicing what I am preaching" in this chapter until I was in my 50s (and I am still working on it). I was able to describe above what people do in their 20s through their 40s because I had similar struggles and challenges at each work cycle stage.

Sure, there were times when I stepped out of my comfort zone and life priorities to follow what Christ was leading me to do, but it was not always pervasive in my life. I am writing this chapter because I have considered myself a serious Christian since the time I became a believer at age 19, yet I too struggled to fully embrace making my work life spiritually significant. I know there are many of you like that.

I was a Vice President at Waste Management the last 14 years of my corporate career — from age 43 to 57 — before entering real estate part-time. I had a demanding job that at times consumed me. But one day, I woke up and what I am writing about in this chapter became crystal clear to me. Obviously, that was the Holy Spirit working on me.

I had been involved in Christian Business Men's Connection (CBMC) when I first started working for Deloitte in Pittsburgh some 30 years earlier. This was a ministry that encouraged business people (in this case men) to share the good news of Jesus Christ with their fellow business people. So, I had a taste early on in my career for living Colossians 3:17.

I decided to do an Internet search for "CBMC Houston," not knowing if there was even a CBMC presence in Houston. To my pleasant surprise, there was a CBMC Houston website. I called the number given and was immediately put in contact with several business people who were a part of the organization in Houston.

To make a long story short, this has led to my involvement with several men in one-on-one evangelism and discipleship relationships. I believe God blessed this simply because I submitted the activities of my job to His will for my life. Since I am now retired from the corporate world and have increased margin, I can and do spend a good deal of my time meeting with men in one-on-one evangelism and discipleship.

Regardless of your work situation, look for the margin that you already have, but may not be taking full advantage of. In my case, it boiled down to acting on a prompting I felt from God to be more intentional about sharing my faith. It took one phone call, and then a series of baby steps, to turn the prompting from God into action and a change in my priorities to be more in line with God's priorities. For you, it probably won't be much different. If your heart is to be more intentional about your faith at work, ask Christ to reveal the next steps for you to do that. It is a prayer that I guarantee He will answer since it is squarely within His will.

You may not need an organization like CBMC to help and encourage you to be the person at work that God has called you to be. However, I do encourage you to have deep fellowship with other like-minded Christians so that you can encourage each other and pray for each other. It is tough to be a lone-ranger Christian. Plus, Jesus Christ has called us into community in order to more effectively live for Him. You can find that community of like-minded Christians either inside or outside a local church, or in both places, as I have done.

When I used to make presentations at work, I would always determine first what the conclusion was — what I wanted my audience to have as the key takeaways and action items. I would then support that conclusion with facts and supporting data to help the listener understand why I had drawn such a conclusion. Likewise, think about what you want your legacy at work to be.

I hope that the most important legacy that you want to leave is the impact for Christ that you had on others. If it is, then start to order your life now around how you will make that outcome a reality. Take the necessary steps now so that you will know you have achieved God's goal for you when you leave your workplace. Make everything that you do, every encounter that you have, subject to Jesus Christ.

CHAPTER 5

Producing Spiritual Fruit

Then Jesus came to them and said,
"All authority in heaven and on earth has been given to Me.
Therefore go and make disciples of all nations,
baptizing them in the name of the Father, and of the Son and
of the Holy Spirit, and teaching them to obey everything I
have commanded you. And surely I am with you always, to the
very end of the age."
Matthew 28:18-20

C hristians have coined these last three verses of the gospel of Matthew as "The Great Commission." At the end of the book of Matthew, Jesus has risen and is now meeting with His disciples in Galilee, where He had told them to go. The disciples were assuredly on the "edge of their seats" wondering what the resurrected Jesus would tell them. He then delivered to them the statement in these three verses, which you could easily subtitle, "The Christian's reason for remaining on earth and not going directly to heaven upon conversion."

I don't know about you, but I have thought a lot about why I am still here on this earth. For the Christian, heaven is his/her ultimate home for eternity. John 5:24 tells us that upon conversion we have crossed over from death to life; we have begun our eternal life. So why doesn't the Christian just go directly to heaven? I think the keynote passage to this chapter (Matthew 28:18-20) gives us the reason.

In Matthew 22:36, a Pharisee wanted to test Jesus by asking this question, *"Teacher, which is the greatest commandment in the Law?"* Jesus replied in this way in verses 37-40:

> *"Love the Lord your God with all your heart and with all your soul and with all your mind. This is the first and greatest commandment. And the second is like it: Love your neighbor as yourself. All the Law and the Prophets hang on these two commandments."*

Jesus gave us the two commandments that should guide our personal conduct while on earth — essentially to love Him and to love others. But in Matthew 28:18-20, He gave us the action steps by which we are to carry out these two great commandments, particularly as it relates to the second one — love your neighbor as yourself. There is no greater act of love than to help lead someone to the eternal decision of accepting Jesus Christ as their personal Savior and surrendering their life to follow Him.

Remember, as I stated in the chapter on *Living a Life of Purpose,* there is no Plan B for God to reach non-Christians with the gospel. Plan A always has been for Christians to reach out to non-Christians with the gospel of Jesus Christ. Christians do that by carrying out the Great Commission. Thus, I would argue that the Great Commission is the Christian's primary reason for staying on this earth.

Have you ever heard people say things like, "I was born to be a quarterback," or "I was born to be a singer," or an actor, or a doctor? You might have said something like that yourself, or maybe something like, "I live to play golf," or "I live to execute the next business deal." Well, if you are a Christian, I have news for you, none of those statements are accurate. The Christian lives on this earth for one primary purpose — to reach others for Christ and to help them then grow in Christ by "making disciples" (Matthew 28:19).

Have you given much thought to how successful you have been at executing your primary reason for remaining on this earth? I recently went to a Men's Retreat where the speaker distributed his "Spiritual Fruit" chart. On it, he had every person who he had ever helped lead to Christ, who they had led to Christ, and who each of them had also discipled to grow in Christ. He also had a "Top Ten" of people who he was praying for to come to Christ. He did not share this so that he could say what a great Christian he was or so that we would all pat him on the back. He shared it to encourage each one of us to think about the kind of spiritual fruit each of us is producing.

To that point, however, there are also some dangers in a person developing their own spiritual fruit chart. It can become a source of unhealthy pride. Alternatively, it could also cause some to "rest on their laurels" and not be pressing on to produce more spiritual fruit.

Thankfully, for most of us, the issue probably is not becoming prideful in our wonderfully long charts. The issue is — do we even have a chart? I am not necessarily talking about whether we have one on paper, but rather whether we have one in substance. Have you helped lead someone to Christ? Have you discipled new believers to grow in their faith? Have you been a spiritual reproducer in that those you have led to Christ or help grow in Christ are now leading others to Christ and discipling others? Do you have a Top Ten of unbelievers that you are praying for and seeking opportunities to connect with so that you can participate in helping lead them to Christ?

Producing spiritual fruit must be intentional. It requires both praying and planning. It requires effort; including effort that may at times be uncomfortable. It requires us to look proactively for where we might make connection points with people. In summary, it requires us to make it an extreme priority. It might be inconvenient where we need to pass on something we like to do because God has given us an opportunity in that moment to produce spiritual fruit that we cannot or should not pass up. But most importantly, it requires a heart set on Christ (Colossians 3:1-2). It also requires us to be connected to the "Vine" Jesus Christ, as John 15:5 describes in the keynote verse heading the chapter on *Spiritual Disciplines*.

A true spiritual reproducer will have a heart like Paul describes in 1 Corinthians 9:19-22:

> *"Though I am free and belong to no one, I make my-self a slave to everyone, to win as many as possible. To the Jew, I became like a Jew, to win the Jews. To those under the law, I became like one under the law (though I myself am not under the law), so as to win those under the law. To those not having the law, I became like one not having the law (though I am not free from God's law, but under Christ's law), so as to win those not having the law. To the weak, I became weak, to win the weak. I have become all things to all men so that by all possible means I might save some."*

Paul was all about producing spiritual fruit. He based his life on it. Christians are called to do the same.

I want to clarify that nothing we do in our own strength produces spiritual fruit. Sure, in obedience, we need to make the efforts to produce spiritual fruit as described in this chapter by being intentional, planning, being willing to be inconvenienced, and praying. But spiritual fruit is ultimately produced by being connected to the Vine. The Christian is merely the branch from the Vine that is used by the Vine to produce fruit.

All praise, honor, and glory rightly belong to Christ the Vine, not to you or me. But with that said, there is no greater privilege or joy in life than to participate in helping someone come to Christ, and then seeing them grow in Christ. Nothing compares to it.

So far, I have not made this chapter very personal. You might be wondering, "What about you Mark? Are you producing spiritual fruit?"

Well, I do not have a documented chart on paper, though I am considering doing so. I have helped in leading several people to Christ, the most recent in the middle of last year. I meet regularly with three men today who are investigating Christ. And I have men who are on my "Top Ten" list that I am praying about for opportunities to share Christ with them. I also regularly pray that God will lead me to other men for whom He wants me to share Christ.

The latter is important to do so that you or I never become stagnant, or overly satisfied, with our present efforts. No matter what activities we are engaged in — work, hobbies, volunteer activities, family time, etc. — we need to always have our "spiritual antennae" up, so as to be alert for the opportunities that Christ gives us as we go about our daily activities. This is referred to by many Christians as "Lifestyle Evangelism."

Just the other day, one of the guys I golf with from time-to-time raised a spiritual issue with me. I play golf with the same group of 35 or so guys about three or four times per month. Before I play, I always ask Christ to help me be aware of relationships that I should develop. Unfortunately, I usually concentrate too much on my bad golf game!

But after about four years of playing golf with these guys, the Lord answered my prayers (despite my sometimes poor attitude resulting from golf) as this man intentionally seemed to raise a spiritual issue with me. I think there is a lesson in perseverance for me as well. We should never stop praying to make a positive impact on people for the sake of Christ, no matter the venue.

In addition to these evangelistic efforts, I currently have regular one-on-one discipleship meetings with four men, where together we are helping each other grow in our relationship with Christ. But the area I know I need to emphasize further is to encourage and help build up the men that I disciple to become disciple-makers themselves. That is a big part of the Great Commission that every serious believer should be emphasizing in their life.

Each Christian needs to be both a first-generation spiritual reproducer, as well as a second-generation spiritual reproducer (those you lead to Christ then lead someone else to Christ, or those you disciple then disciple someone else), and third-generation reproducer, etc. The man who led the retreat I referred to above had a spiritual fruit chart that went several spiritual generations deep.

Before closing this chapter, I want to share with you the final words of Jesus to His disciples, and to us, as recorded in Matthew 28:20, *"And surely I am with you always, to the very end of the age."*

You may feel that you are not naturally "gifted" or equipped to lead someone to Christ. However, Jesus did not limit The Great Commission to preachers, teachers, evangelists, or others with a special gift. By staying connected to the Vine, we allow His Spirit to work through our perceived weaknesses.

Being a spiritual reproducer might not always be easy. There will likely be some uncomfortable or awkward moments. You might feel like you have failed with one or more people that you felt led to become involved with. But always remember that the "results" are not up to you. The results are produced by the Vine; you and I are just a branch.

It may be that your efforts with one person are just a link in the chain to bring that person to Christ; possibly through an encouraging word, or maybe by earnestly praying for someone to come to Christ. Or, it may be that you are the final link in the chain to help lead that person to pray to receive Christ as Savior and Lord. Regardless of the specific role you or I might play in the life of the unbeliever, our job is obedience to the call, not the production of results.

And no matter what we face in our efforts at producing spiritual fruit, we are given this great promise by Jesus in Matthew 28:20 that He is always with us, to the very end of the age. Knowing that, I encourage you to do your best to take spiritual risks and step out in faith as an evangelistic disciple-maker. At the end of your life and mine, I am certain that we will never regret that we did.

CHAPTER 6

Loving Others Not Like You

Get rid of all bitterness, rage and anger, brawling and slander,
along with every form of malice.
Be kind and compassionate to one another,
forgiving each other,
just as in Christ God forgave you.
Ephesians 4:31-32

It would be an understatement to say that there are a lot of people who are not like you. There are people that do not share your values or your political affiliation. They probably do not like the same sports teams as you and may not have the same interests in music. They may also not share the same faith as you. The list of differences with our fellow human beings can go on and on.

When you look at the political landscape in America, it is clear that there is a lot of division. And not just division based on political, social, or religious differences. Today we are witnessing in society all the things described in this chapter's keynote passage in Ephesians 4:31-32 — bitterness, rage, anger, brawling, slander, and yes, every kind of malice. The world is spinning out of control, as life moves at a fast pace, and people around us just do not seem to "get it" as we think they should.

For instance, not long ago, I accidentally tapped the side view mirror of the car parked next to me with my door as I was getting in my truck. No harm was done to the mirror, but the other driver came storming out in rage. It appears many of us live on the edge of anger and even rage.

For the committed Christian, we struggle with being true to biblical standards while still loving those who blatantly appear to be outside that standard. I recently heard of a situation where a man was leading a small group discussion centered on the Bible. For one particular session, he decided to open the discussion by giving the people in the group the opportunity to ask any question that they had, regardless of the topic. The first person, who was a lesbian, asked whether or not she was going to hell because she was a lesbian. Well, so much for a first "lay-up" question!

The leader soon realized that the person asking the question felt judged by Christians she associated with. She had heard that the Bible does not condone homosexuality, and she felt judged, leading to anger. Rather than address that specific issue with the woman, the leader explained that every person has multiple issues that need the redeeming love of Christ. The leader was in no position to judge the eternal destiny of that person. That is up to God for every single one of us. But he was in a position to empathize with her, because like her he was a fellow sinner in need of a Savior, no matter what the issue might be.

It is not the Christian's job to judge a person's "sin level." That is thankfully up to God and not you or me. It is every person's responsibility to investigate the Word of God and judge for themselves how they will respond to it. I believe that the Bible is the infallible Word of God. It is my objective source of truth. As best I can, I attempt to live my life in accordance with what it says. As a believer, I am called to share the truth of the Word and encourage others to come to faith. But as a believer, I am not to be in the business of judging a person's level of sin and certainly not judging their eternal destiny.

The issue for each of us is not the level of sin. The issue is what Romans 3:23 says, *"All have sinned and fall short of the glory of God."* It does not matter what the sin is or the perceived level of the sin. Every single one of us needs forgiveness, because every single one of us has sinned, and has sinned multiple times. The leader of that discussion group needs a Savior just as much as the woman who asked the question.

I have a news flash for you. You are not the judge of all people, nor am I. Rather, we are called to what the keynote verse says in Ephesians 4:32, *"Be kind and compassionate to one another, forgiving each other, just as in Christ God forgave you."*

The apostle Paul is not talking about just the people that we like. In fact, he is likely talking more about the people that we do not like. Jesus said in Matthew 5:44, *"Love your enemies and pray for those who persecute you."* He goes on to say in verse 46, *"If you love those who love you, what reward will you get? Are not even the tax collectors doing that?"* (Keep in mind that the tax collector was the most hated profession of the people during the time Jesus walked the earth.)

Think about how different the world would be if everyone acted as commanded in these verses — to be kind, compassionate, forgiving, and to love your enemies. We would not recognize this world. Actually, this world would likely look a lot more like heaven looks.

Stop for a moment and think about the things about people that have upset you over the last few days. In the grand scheme of things, how many of the issues you are thinking about now really matter? If you are like me, and honestly answer that question, probably not too many. As I would constantly tell my children when they were growing up (and sometimes still today), learn to take the "high road" and not wallow in petty disagreements. Let go of your "right" to get angry and instead extend grace and forgiveness.

I sometimes watch or listen to the news and get frustrated with what some people are saying. Honestly, it is often hard to understand how people can have some of the viewpoints they have. But you know, they would likely think the same thing about me. Rather than hate that person for their views, maybe I could instead try to understand why they have the views that they do. But more importantly, I should look at that person and understand that they are a precious gift from God, created in His image, and with whom God desires an intimate relationship. That person is equally as valuable to God as I am.

Think about that for a moment. Every person who has ever lived is equally as valuable to God as you are. God desires that each person comes to faith in Christ and enters into a personal relationship with Him (1 Timothy 2:3-4). If God thinks that about every single one of our fellow men and women, what right do we have to think differently than God about them? The answer is that we do not have that right.

Often, a person acts in a less than optimal way because of the circumstances of their life behind the scenes — things that are out of our immediate viewpoint. Maybe it is a fight with his/her spouse or children, a death in the family, a difficult boss at work, or a lost job. The circumstances can be endless. But how much better the world would be, and we would be, if we would extend grace to that person in a way that we would like to receive grace if we were facing one or more of these same behind-the-scenes issues.

Extending grace is not a common practice in today's society. When someone does it, it is at least a surprise and sometimes a downright shock. Recently, I encouraged someone to forgive a perceived wrong of another. When I shared what I had encouraged with another person close to both people who were in the dispute, this other person acted like that was a reaction so out of the norm that he would have never even considered it. When you extend grace, you live uncommonly. It is not a natural reaction of mankind. But for the Christian, it should be more commonplace than it is today.

When you extend grace, you open the possibility of that person receiving grace and desiring to give it to others. Indeed, you open the possibility to share Christ with that person. Which is better — extending grace and opening the possibility of another person coming to Christ, or not extending grace and making sure that you have made your clearly accurate point and put that person in his/her place?

I will close this chapter by quoting from Romans 12:18," *If it is possible, as far as it depends on you, live at peace with everyone. "* It is not always going to be possible to live at peace with everyone you encounter. The apostle Paul acknowledges that in this verse when he says, *"If it is possible."* But if it *"depends on you, "* as the verse says, we should make every effort to see the other person as God sees that person, extend grace, live at peace with that person, and then watch Christ act in that person's life.

CHAPTER 7

Disciple-Making

And the things you have heard me say
in the presence of many witnesses
entrust to reliable men who will also be
qualified to teach others.
2 Timothy 2:2

I have been meeting with a young man (relatively speaking, at least compared to me) consistently for the last eight years. For much of that time, Jason and I met on a weekly basis, though recently we have begun to meet every two or three weeks. We have been through a lot together. During the time that I have known Jason, he has gotten married, he and his wife, Courtney, have had two sons, he has gone through a medical scare, and he has changed jobs twice.

As for me, I have left the corporate world for real estate, my three daughters have married, and Cindy and I now have five grandchildren. I met Jason on an airplane where we struck up a conversation. I contacted him shortly thereafter, met him for lunch, and offered to meet with him in one-on-one discipleship. Maybe to your surprise and mine, Jason said "yes" and our friendship began.

I just used the word "friendship," but it is much more than that. We have discussed the deep issues of life, and have shared in each other's successes, failures, and challenges. Cindy and I have spent time with Jason and Courtney, and their children. We have been through health scares together, important career changes, and times where each of us has been spiritually challenged. We have looked at what Scripture is saying to us and have memorized Scripture together. We have also had fun together, playing golf, and attending events and retreats together. We know each other's strengths and weaknesses.

Through it all though, the one dominant theme of our friendship has been helping each other to grow in the relationship each of us has with Christ. I have observed that Jason's relationship with Christ has evolved from being initially solidified to the point where he now attempts to make his life more about Christ than himself. This one-on-one discipleship experience has been great for both of us.

Going back in time over 30 years ago, I too was discipled in my 20s and 30s when I lived in Newport News, VA. Much like I did with Jason, a man by the name of Frank Satchell asked me to join him every Saturday morning for Bible study, prayer, and on-going discussions of how each of us could grow as Christ-followers. We met nearly every Saturday morning for eleven years until I moved to Houston.

Frank has not been in my life regularly now for over 20 years, but we do see each other every few years. He and his wife, Elizabeth, have traveled halfway across the country to two of my daughters' weddings, and we have made a point to stop in and see each other periodically. When we do see each other, or talk on the phone, it is like we never stopped meeting.

The deep fellowship that we developed over those eleven years remains and will last into eternity. If I ever have an important need to be met, I would call Frank first, even though we have not lived in the same city for 23 years and we are half a country apart.

Disciple-making is not for the faint-hearted. Disciple-making also cannot be reduced to a program. Rather, it is an organic process between two people. The one being discipled needs to be willing and teachable, and the discipler needs to see his/her investment of time in the process as important in relation to everything else in his/her life. (I will call the discipler "Paul" from this point forward and the one being discipled "Timothy," patterned after the Paul/Timothy relationship in the New Testament.) The Paul and the Timothy can be male or female, though it is almost always better and more appropriate that the relationships be developed between two people of the same gender.

Frankly, in my experience, one-on-one discipleship among Christians is not all that common. It is not as exciting as evangelism, where many churches and Christians focus their attention. That is not to say that evangelism is not critical, because it absolutely is. But Jesus told us to "make disciples" in Matthew 28:19. A new believer's experience with Christ should not stop at conversion. Rather, it should continue in discipleship to the point where the new believer can then evangelize and disciple someone else (see the 2 Timothy 2:2 Scripture reference at the beginning of this chapter). It is the process of spiritual multiplication that Jesus Christ ordained for Christ-followers to do.

The process of discipleship is rarely a church program, but is instead an organic process. Just like mentoring cannot be prescribed in the business world, discipleship must come about because two people are led by the Lord to enter such a relationship. It takes mature believers who understand the criticality of Christ's command in Matthew 28:18-20, and those who want to be discipled because they truly desire to grow in their relationship with Jesus Christ.

Every Christian is called to be a reproducer of the faith. Jesus Christ has made that clear. As I have mentioned in other chapters in this book, God has no Plan B for the proliferation of the gospel and the continuance of the church — the body of Christ.

So, what does a discipleship relationship look like? Frankly, they are all different and are conducted at various levels of transparency. At its core, discipleship includes the study of the Bible and prayer, plus the discipline of Scripture memory. Memorizing Scripture is important so that the Timothy in the discipleship relationship can begin to incorporate the Word of God into his/her life in an intimate and practical way. Life brings us daily challenges that should often be met by readily applying memorized Scripture to the situation. It brings to life the importance of the Word of God into the Timothy's life.

Beyond these core discipleship activities, discipleship really comes to life by dealing with the issues and challenges of life that both the Timothy and the Paul will invariably face. This requires the willingness to be transparent with each other and to work through these challenges and issues together, as both seek the Lord's guidance to do so.

It also means that the Paul and the Timothy will likely spend time with each other's family members, as well as attending functions together and just plain having fun together. Think about what Jesus did with His twelve disciples, and His core group of three disciples — He spent time with them. He taught them through all the challenges they faced. He let them observe how He faced challenges. He was deeply and intimately involved in their lives.

I am sure Jesus had plenty of one-on-one time with His disciples that were not recorded in the Scriptures. But note that another form of discipleship can take place in a group, just like Jesus modeled for us with His disciples. In many churches, this is how discipleship takes place — through small groups. The challenge of these groups is that the leaders of these groups should be mature believers, focused on the spiritual development of the members of these groups.

Other challenges of group discipleship are involving every person in the life of the group in a significant way and developing a level of transparency and intimacy among group members. Group members need to be willing to truly do life together and share with each other in ways like the one-on-one discipleship model.

Acts 1:8 addresses another discipleship model. So far in this chapter, we have discussed the discipleship of people in our tighter sphere of influence; referred to in Acts 1:8 as our "Jerusalem." There also may be people that we can influence in our "Judea and Samaria" as well as those "to the ends of the earth." These last two groups, out of our tight sphere of influence, are typically impacted more by evangelistic efforts through domestic and foreign mission activity, rather than discipleship activity.

Back to one-on-one discipleship relationships. Where do we find such relationships? I would argue that you find them right where you are. My current and recent discipleship relationships have come primarily from work associates. They have also come from business groups, people I met at church, and as I previously described, with a person I met on an airplane.

Being in real estate, I have a little more flexibility than most, so I currently have seven people with whom I am actively engaged in either an evangelistic or discipleship relationship, or both. But all these relationships developed from natural activities that I was already engaged in. I have just tried to be sensitive to the leading of the Holy Spirit as He prompts me to engage in a relationship.

Sometimes, it will be plainly obvious that you need to enter into a one-on-one relationship with someone. As I wrote about in the chapter on *Making the Most of Every Opportunity*, an example of this was when a work associate from years ago texted with a real estate question, then ended the text with "my life is in a shambles."

If you are a "Paul" in a discipleship relationship now, I encourage you to actively pursue your own faith so that you can better pour your life into your "Timothy" and develop him/her as a disciple of Christ. If you are a mature believer and not currently discipling another person, I encourage you to pray about it so that Christ might lead you into such a relationship. If you are a believer that has never been discipled, ask Christ to reveal to you if there is someone that might fill that Paul role in your life. If you are an unbeliever, be willing to engage with a Christian with whom you respect and try to get to know better what makes that person "tick."

Regardless of your current status in relation to disciple-making, I hope this chapter has inspired you in some way to go on the God-ordained discipleship journey.

CHAPTER 8

Becoming a Patriarch
or Matriarch

Who is wise and understanding among you?
Let him show it by his good life,
by deeds done in the humility that comes from wisdom.
James 3:13

In the last several years, I unexpectedly realized that God had given me a measure of wisdom to share with others. This wisdom is not always revelatory, but the fact is that I have lived for a longer period than most people that I regularly meet with. As a result, I have had the opportunity to have more life experiences than they have. I have had my share of failures, and a few successes, but hopefully along the way, Christ has taught me something through all those experiences that just might be worth sharing.

In preparation for writing this chapter, I looked up the definition of a patriarch and I did not quite find what I was looking for. In addition to the Biblical reference of a patriarch being one of the founding fathers of the Hebrew nation (e.g., Abraham), I found two definitions that were not exactly flattering: 1) the oldest member or representative of a group, and 2) a venerable old man. Admittedly, I did not exactly like the emphasis on "old!"

I then looked up the definition of a matriarch and found more what I thought I would find: "a mother who is head and ruler of her family and descendants." No reference to age for women. Daniel Webster was not a dummy!

In sifting through these definitions, the thing that genuinely struck me was the reference to "descendants." A patriarch and a matriarch have a keen sense that what they do and say today may have an impact for generations to come. And importantly, they deeply care about that impact.

So, if you are age 50+ this chapter just might be for you. On the other hand, there is actually no minimum age requirement to take on this patriarchal/matriarchal role. It is truthfully more of an attitude adjustment. It is the realization that what God has taught you over the years might truly be helpful to those close to you, and to those near and dear to you. One caution though — just because you feel God calling you into this role does not mean you have "arrived." You and I are still learners. We always need to stay FAT — Faithful, Available, and Teachable. God is still in the business of refining us to the day that we die.

Maybe one of the first times I realized that I had a patriarchal role to play was when my youngest daughter was going through difficulties in college. I started writing her notes, primarily based on Scripture, to encourage her through some tough times. Eventually, this morphed into a daily occurrence when I would tell her in an email what I learned from my daily Quiet Time (see the chapter on *Spiritual Disciplines* for further information on the benefits of having a daily Quiet Time routine).

After doing this for a while, and seeing the positive influence on her, I realized that there was no reason not to share these with my other three grown children. So, for the last 10+ years, I have sent all my children these daily Quiet Time "commentaries," rarely missing a day. Along the way, I have added my sons-in-law and a few friends that requested to be included as well. One of my sons-in-law even forwards the daily note to his ex-boss as a source of encouragement.

As a side note, in addition to sharing what I have learned from Christ as I read His Word, hopefully offering practical advice and strategies to my family, I do this so that I might set an example for them to daily open their Bibles and hear from God. Part of being a patriarch is not just sharing the God-given wisdom that you have attained over the years, it is also about example setting.

Some of you may be thinking right now that you really do not have anything special to say to your family or those close around you. But, if you are someone who has been in earnest pursuit of Jesus Christ for several years, I would challenge such thinking. It is impossible for you to consistently pursue Christ and not have learned something from Him over the years that you can share with others. You undoubtedly have both God-given wisdom and stories to share that would be helpful to less "seasoned" members of your family. Plus, you may not think it, but probably most of the members of your family expect you to be a patriarch or matriarch. They actually want to hear what you have to say, even though they may not verbalize or request it.

Maybe you have been a Christian for only a few years, or you have not been that believer who has earnestly pursued God through His Word and prayer. If so, I would encourage you to start now, as it is never too late. God might have something He wants to teach you and impress upon your heart tomorrow morning that you need to share with others. Do not miss out on that. In addition, you also have a lot of life experiences behind you. You may not have looked at those experiences at the time from the same perspective that you have now. However, the new perspective you now have on any mistakes you might have made could prove invaluable to others. It just might keep them from heading down the wrong path themselves.

Another thing that I do in the role of a patriarch is to volunteer at the local crisis pregnancy center. My role there is to speak with the young men who come in with their girlfriends or wives. This may not be a direct patriarch role to my family, but volunteering in this way is because of the realization that God gave me this patriarch role to play. I get to spend about a half-hour with each young man that comes in. I have two goals in each of those brief meetings — to help them through their situation in whatever way that I can and to share the saving grace of Jesus Christ with them. Very few of these young men come to faith in that short time span, but I know that I may just be one link in a chain of encounters and experiences that might bring them to Christ.

These young men need to hear the truth, not the lies that society tells them. I have heard quite a few sensational stories, so I have learned to take those encounters in stride. But one thing that is consistent across the board is that most of these young men do not see how they can keep from having sex outside of marriage. They view it as an inevitable thing, almost like they are not in control of their own bodies. In essence, they have "set the bar low" for themselves.

I tell them to stop setting the bar low and start taking control of their own sexual promiscuity. I tell them to raise the bar for themselves and challenge themselves to do the right thing. (Of course, it is much more possible to do this when you have the power of the Holy Spirit living in you.) Part of being a patriarch is also being the person willing to challenge others to a higher standard. Patriarchs oftentimes cannot sit idly by.

Being a patriarch is not being a "know it all." You are not going to have the solution to every problem. And even if you think you have that solution, make sure it is a solution that is motivated by Christ and not just your own personal opinion. Being a patriarch, or a matriarch, is simply having a mindset that God has given you wisdom that He wants you to share, particularly with those close to you.

I sometimes find that when I am sharing things with family members or those close to me, I feel almost like it is not really me talking. I am saying things that I did not know I had the wisdom to share. Obviously, that is the work of the Holy Spirit in the patriarch/matriarch. But without the initial mindset to share with others, you will never share what God wants to put in your heart for the benefit of those around you. What a missed opportunity for the sake of the Kingdom of God!

One other thing — whether you embrace the role of patriarch or matriarch, you are often one just by virtue of your age. For instance, it is hard to be a grandparent and not be a patriarch or matriarch. The question is: are you going to embrace the role or seek to avoid it? The chapter on *Making the Most of Every Opportunity* has some helpful advice for those embarking or continuing on a patriarch or matriarch journey.

When we reject the role that God wants us to have, who knows how many missed opportunities we might have had; and not just for our sake, but for the sake of others. I once heard a sermon where the pastor talked about all the unopened "blessing boxes" that Christians will see once they get to heaven. If only we have the courage to step out in faith, we could not only receive these blessings but could also be the instrument God uses to bless others while on this earth.

Embrace the role and tremendous opportunity of being the patriarch or matriarch that God wants you to take on. This will be a new chapter in your life that will undoubtedly yield spiritually significant results in you and in the lives of those around you.

CHAPTER 9

Trusting Christ
in Uncertain Times

Set your minds on things above, not on earthly things.
Colossians 3:2

What do you do when faced with a situation that you do not like or is uncomfortable? I don't know about you, but I know what I do. I look for the fastest way out of the situation. My first inclination is to take control. Sometimes, a detailed analysis may be required to determine the best "exit strategy" from the situation. It may also be helpful to do the old "pros and cons" analysis to determine the best course of action. No matter how you or I address uncomfortable situations in life, it is highly likely that the first reaction that we have is to get out of the situation as quickly, and as pain-free, as possible.

Of course, while we are trying to determine our exit strategy, we usually find it both natural and important to worry about the situation — this is particularly true when the situation involves another human being whom we cannot control. Whether you are a Christian or not, everyone instinctively knows that worry does not accomplish anything except maybe adding even more stress to the situation and increasing one's blood pressure. Jesus Christ made it clear in Matthew 6:27 when He said, ***"Who of you by worrying can add a single hour to his life?"*** You can reference the chapter on *Don't Worry* for further ideas on reducing the worry in your life.

Is there another, better approach to take when faced with the various challenges that life brings? Have you ever looked at your challenging situation and said, "This is a great opportunity for me to exercise my faith and watch Christ work in my life?" Instead of worrying about whatever it is you might be facing, view every challenging situation in life as an opportunity to draw closer to Christ, and to give Him glory.

Think about it. At the end of your life, what is going to be the most important thing to you? It won't be that you conquered a life situation by exercising a great strategy. Instead, I am certain that you will want to have the absolute closest, most intimate relationship with Jesus Christ that you can have.

I want to make a confession. About 6-7 years ago, I was experiencing severe leg cramps in both of my legs. In fact, the day before I was to go to the hospital to check out what the issue was, I was lying in bed with my legs shaking uncontrollably for more than an hour. My wife, Cindy, had to hold down my legs to keep them from shaking. I began to fear that I was experiencing the first signs of a neuromuscular disease, like muscular dystrophy.

I can tell you that during the next 18 hours all I thought about was what the results of that test would be the next morning. I was even thinking about how I might deal with it the rest of my life, and how my life as I knew it might change. I worried I might not be able to walk in the near future and would certainly not be able to play golf very much longer. I also thought, is there something *I* can do to slow the process?

You know, I prayed during those 18 hours. Primarily, I prayed that God would keep the diagnosis from being something bad, something that might eventually be life threatening. Though I may have prayed a little that Christ would show me something through this challenge, that was certainly not my first thought, nor even the dominant theme, of my prayers. Frankly, it is a little embarrassing to reveal my thought process through that challenge.

Immediately after the test was administered that morning I received the results from the doctor. Instead of having a life-threatening neuro-muscular disease, I had a lower back disc issue (L4/L5). Now, back issues are not fun in and of themselves, but they are not generally life threatening. And while there was an immediate sense of relief, there was also an immediate sense of shame. I thought of myself as a strong believer, who was ready to leave this world if God called me heavenward. Yet, here I was a self-described strong believer who allowed fear and a good sense of imagination about my potential malady to take hold of me.

I asked God for forgiveness for my lack of trust and I vowed never to let fear overtake me when it came to medical issues. Not only was I a poor witness to my wife, but I had severely let myself down and, most importantly, Jesus Christ. I hope and pray that if ever faced with a similar situation in the future that I will respond much differently.

What I have described is just one kind of challenge that each of us might face in the near or distant future. In fact, each of us is certain to face a difficult circumstance or situation that might challenge our faith. But instead of wanting the situation to "just be over and resolved," isn't a better reaction to look around and see what Christ might be trying to do in your life and mine? Remember, if the thesis is accurate that the most important thing a person can possess is a deep, personal relationship with Jesus Christ, then it only makes sense that we should allow every challenge we face to draw us closer to Christ. The possibility of an improved relationship with Him should always take precedence over the necessity to put the situation behind us.

The question becomes — do we want the Healer Himself, Jesus Christ, more than we want Him to heal us? In other words, do we want the Healer in our lives more than the healing, or the benefit He might provide to us? Do we want the Giver of all good things, Jesus Christ, more than we want the gifts that He might provide to us? The bottom line is — do we want a more intimate relationship with Christ now and into eternity more than we want the benefits He might choose to give us in this life alone?

Here is what I have come to understand is the definition of an exciting, meaningful life. It is one where we are willing to go on an exciting journey with the Creator of the Universe through His Son Jesus Christ. It is when we can look for, and then actually see, Christ at work in our lives. We cannot see that, though, if all we are worried about is exiting ourselves from a difficult situation we might be in.

Recall the biblical story of Jonah and the great fish. Jonah, while still in the body of the great fish, makes an insightful statement in Jonah 2:8, ***"Those who cling to worthless idols forfeit the grace that could be theirs."***

When we are focused on a difficult life challenge, and not on our relationship with Christ, we do just that — we forfeit the grace that could be ours. I shudder to think about all of the forfeitures I have made in my life because I was focused on me and not on Christ. What about you?

In my experiences with the men I have discipled, few of them initially focused on improving their relationships with Christ instead of concentrating on finding ways to quickly solving their problems. But when they give it more thought, they often saw the merit of placing Christ over problems.

Jesus said in John 10:10 that, *"I have come that they might have life, and have it more abundantly."* What is the most abundant life you can have? I would argue that it is a life where everything you do involves the person of Jesus Christ. And in every crisis you face, you watch Him work in that crisis to grow you and others around you.

This will also undoubtedly increase the peace and joy you have as you see the positive difference Christ is making in you. I will state it emphatically again; the most important thing we can do in life is growing in our intimacy with Jesus Christ. It is the thing that we will most value at the end of our lives.

In order to prepare ourselves to live this abundant life, by inviting Christ into each challenge in our journey of life, we must first prepare ourselves on a daily basis to react in such a manner. The keynote verse of this chapter is Colossians 3:2, *"Set your minds on things above, not on earthly things."* Just like the athlete trains for the important game, we must train ourselves to "have our minds set on things above" before the challenges in life hit us.

The only way I know to do this is to have a significant daily quiet time of Scripture reading and prayer. In addition, 1 Thessalonians 5:17 tells us to "pray continually," maintaining a constant awareness of Christ in our lives. Of course, having an accountability partner(s) you can share life with and being involved in regular fellowship and worship with a body of believers can also help prepare you for the storms of life. When life's challenges come, we will then be better equipped to first look for Christ at work, rather than first look for our way out.

I know, in many ways, the reaction that I am proposing to the challenges in each of our lives is easier said than done. Admittedly, it is easier for me to write this than to put it into practice. But never lower your standard for what you want to become in Jesus Christ. Just because it is hard, that does not mean that you cannot do it through the power of

Jesus Christ. I hope that you will one day be able to attest to this by the way you react to the next significant challenge in your life.

CHAPTER 10

Humility

Blessed are the poor in spirit,
for theirs is the kingdom of heaven.
Matthew 5:3

There is no substitute for *it* in the life of a true believer in Jesus Christ. **_Humility_** is at the core of every serious believer.

Think about it. Can you come to a saving faith in Jesus Christ without humility? Of course not. To be a Christian, you must admit that you have a need. And that need for every person that has ever lived is to have their sin problem resolved. It does not matter how good you are in the eyes of others or yourself. Everyone has a serious sin problem! Each one of us is in *desperate* need of a Savior.

I remember as a 19-year-old, before I became a Christian, I thought I was a pretty good guy. If the truth were known, compared to most of my friends, I probably was. But in whose eyes and by whose standard? Of course, I fell far short of God's standard for my life — perfection (Mathew 5:48). I was in desperate need of a Savior. But you know what? Even though I eventually came to that conclusion myself, prompted by the work of the Holy Spirit in my life, having to admit this was the biggest barrier to me finally turning my life over to Christ. I did not want to admit that I had a need. But I did – a HUGE need!

So, I would argue that humility is the cornerstone trait that a person must possess, at least in the moment, to come to Christ. But it is also the most important trait that we must possess to really live for Christ. The absence of humility is self-reliance. Self-reliance leads to the absence of Christ. Any time that you or I think that we can go it alone, look out! Doing so eliminates the greatest power source in life. Sure, we may temporarily achieve a "win" here and there, but those wins will be few and far between and will certainly not last the test of time.

Why does anyone not see a need for humility in their life? Shouldn't it be obvious that everyone needs humility in light of an honest comparison to Jesus Christ? But therein may be the problem. We are often not comparing ourselves to the standards of Jesus Christ as documented in the Scriptures. Rather, we are comparing ourselves to our neighbors, co-workers, or even fellow church members. If that is the standard for my life, even I can sometimes look good. But that is clearly not the right standard. You and I are not only in desperate need of Christ for salvation, but we are also in desperate need of Him to help us live effective, Christ-honoring lives.

To be honest, I am a rather self-assured person. I have lived long enough and had enough experiences that I am not too surprised by most things. In reality, my Christian faith helps me to be self- assured because I know that no matter what happens, Christ will see me through. That is certainly a major blessing of being a Christian — to be confident that Christ will walk with you no matter what comes your way. It helps me to be self-assured and much less afraid.

But in the last year, I have begun to pray every day that Christ will make me more humble. Even if my confidence is based in Him, I do not want to appear to others to be overly self-assured. Doing so can stifle a conversation and prevent deeper relationships from forming with others. Almost no one wants to be around a know-it-all. I do not want to miss out on what God might have planned for me (and others) because I lack humility.

When I was working in the corporate world in the early and middle parts of my career, I was very concerned about being completely prepared and ready to answer every question or objection that might come my way in a meeting. I wanted others to know that I "knew my stuff." And I certainly did not want to be embarrassed because I did not know something I should have known. I wanted people to walk out of each meeting impressed by ME.

But as I began to better grasp the concept of Christian humility, I became much less concerned about impressing others. In reality, it was very freeing. Don't get me wrong here. I prepared the same in the latter stages of my career as I had done earlier. I just grasped humility better. It was okay not to know everything. It was okay to learn from others. When you take this approach with others, it frees them up too. Relationships begin to be possible — maybe even relationships that will one day help someone come to Christ.

Personalizing it a bit for you, what is the area of your life where you need to be more humble? Is it your job, your marriage, humility toward your kids, politics? Perhaps even the way that you approach living the Christian life (maybe you think you have that all figured out too)? Or is it a predominant thing in your life that needs addressing, just like I have expressed about me?

I encourage you to stop right now and pray about it. Ask God to show you where you need greater humility and the specific steps you can take to be a humble person. Lacking humility is a tiring way to live life. I encourage you to give it up. You do not need to be the smartest, best man or woman in the room every time. What you need to be is the best representative of Jesus Christ that you can be in every situation that you encounter.

As I write this book, we live in a polarizing time from a political perspective. Those on both the right and the left are encouraged to be as far right or left as their political persuasions will take them. There seems very little room anymore for the middle ground. I am not trying to make a political statement here or trying to cause you to be less passionate about your views. However, I am encouraging you to try to apply a little humility to your arguments, and more importantly, to your relationships.

As completely right as you think you might be, it might be possible that the other person has at least a measure of a good point. And even if they do not, a humble approach to that person might just lead to a real relationship with that person, and that relationship could be the beginning of you sharing your faith with them. Let me ask you, is it more important that you win the political argument, or that you develop a relationship that could potentially lead that person into heaven? I don't think I need to answer that question for you.

Making it closer to home — for those of you who are Moms and Dads, have you ever told your children that you blew it and you are sorry? Have you ever told your spouse the same thing? Stop trying to be something that you can never be on your own. You are not perfect, and I guarantee you everyone around you knows it! And, undoubtedly, Jesus Christ knows exactly why you really ought to be humble before Him.

In Matthew 18:1, the disciples of Jesus ask Him, "Who is the greatest in the kingdom of heaven?" He responds in verses 3 and 4 with: *"I tell you the truth, unless you change and become like little children, you will never enter the kingdom of heaven. Therefore, whoever humbles himself like this child is the greatest in the kingdom of heaven."*

Jesus is emphasizing that to begin a personal relationship with Him every person needs to come to Him in complete humility. Jesus is telling His disciples that rather than worry about who is the greatest, they should worry about who is the most humble.

One story before I end this chapter. About ten years before my corporate career came to an end, I had a business argument with a fellow Vice President at Waste Management. It was not a heated argument, but let's just say it was "spirited." I walked away from that meeting a little "ticked," and not understanding of why my colleague could not see things my way (of course the "right way").

I decided to avoid that colleague for the next day, and maybe weeks, as I did not want to be around him. However, my colleague had a different idea. He called me a few days later and asked me to come to his office. My first reaction was, "Why don't you come to my office?" Fortunately, I did not verbalize that! When I got there, he graciously asked me to sit down and then proceeded to apologize to me for being wrong in the argument and the way that he had handled himself. This man was not known for being humble, but here he was showing the supposedly mature believer (me) how to act with humility.

To this day, I could not tell you what that argument was about. Could it really have been that important? But I can tell you one thing. I know how I felt at that moment and still do to this day about that man, even though our paths have gone different ways. I was humbled by his humbleness. He showed me what it was like to be humble in the workplace, and in life. This man had many detractors at Waste Management, but I can assure you from that day forward that I was not one of them. No matter what he did, after his display of humility toward me, he got a "pass" from me. That is the power of humility.

Back to the keynote verse of this chapter—Matthew 5:3, ***"Blessed are the poor in spirit, for theirs is the kingdom of heaven."*** Simply put, look what the "poor in spirit," or the humble, receive — the kingdom of heaven. Now, that is certainly referring to eternity, but I believe it also has application for each of our lives while on this earth. If you want blessings in this life on earth, you will be humble.

CHAPTER 11

Grumbling, Gratitude, and Unwholesome Talk

Do everything without complaining or arguing.
Philippians 2:14

ince becoming a Christian 43 years ago, I have observed two rather consistent and subtle behaviors of believers that are closely related but are not necessarily "becoming" to the cause of Christ.

The first relates to how a believer is to speak to others. Ephesians 4:29 says, ***"Do not let any unwholesome talk come out of your mouths, but only what is helpful for building others up according to their needs, that it may benefit those who listen."*** The other one relates to the keynote verse of this chapter, Philippians 2:14, ***"Do everything without complaining or arguing."***

These are things that Christians do not talk about a lot. However, they can have a very significant impact on the way a believer thinks, lives, and bears witness to the non-believing world.

As a rule, most people are not impressed with negativity. Most people are also not impressed with someone who is not encouraging and prefers to say a coarse or discouraging word instead of an encouraging word. I know few Christians who have not struggled in these areas, including myself. But I would advocate that these character traits are more important to the quality of the Christian's relationship with Christ and the spread of the gospel than most of us would like to acknowledge.

I will comment first on Ephesians 4:29. How would you and I define "unwholesome talk?" From my vantage point, the best way to evaluate unwholesome talk is this, "Would I say what I am about to say if Jesus Christ were standing right in front of me?" Most likely, this evaluation standard would limit my vocabulary a bit!

I have heard the argument from well-meaning Christians that they need to speak a little rough in front of non-believers so that they can relate well with them. They use the argument Paul used in relating to non-believers in 1 Corinthians 9:19-23 *("I make myself a slave to everyone to win as many as possible.")*.

Certainly, the believer is called to live among non-believers in a relatable way. That is what Paul was talking about. But he was not talking about compromising beliefs, character, or even speech. My observation is that some believers use this "relatable" argument to justify the language they used before coming to Christ and then continue to use because they have not allowed their speech to be subject to the Lordship of Christ.

When we come to Christ, we are to give every aspect of our life to Him, including the way that we talk. Second Corinthians 5:17 says that the new believer is a *"new creation; the old has gone, the new has come."*

Non-believers want us to be relatable, but even if they specifically realize it or not, they also want us to display a real difference in the way that we live. They need to see something attractive in the Christian that they want too, something where they see that faith makes a difference in the Christian's life.

Language can be a real and clear difference-maker. If you used to use coarse language, and now you do not, you are displaying the "new creation" that you are, and the non-believer sees it. I would suggest that you are not less relatable, but instead more interesting and attractive to non-believers.

Curiously, some of the Christians I know do not use coarse language just to be relatable among non-Christians. They also use coarse language when speaking just among believers. Think about that for a moment. Is there ever a good reason to use coarse language among believers? Even if you think you are being relatable among non-believers, which I would argue is at least mildly misguided, you are not adding anything to a discussion among believers when using coarse language. I will say it again, Jesus Christ came to transform us in every area of our life, including our speech.

The book of James gives us two very stern warnings about the way that we speak. James 1:26 tells us this: *"If anyone considers himself religious and yet does not keep a tight rein on his tongue, he deceives himself and his religion is worthless."*

Further, James 3:6 tells us, *"The tongue also is a fire, a world of evil among the parts of the body. It corrupts the whole person, sets the whole course of his life on fire, and is itself set on fire by hell."*

These verses make it very clear that the way we speak not only impacts the Christian's witness to the non-believing world, but it also greatly impacts the quality of the Christian's relationship with Jesus Christ. Suffice it to say that Jesus Christ greatly values the way that we speak. The Word of God makes it clear that our speech has the impact of affecting virtually every area of our lives — either positively or negatively. We get to choose which way it will be.

As noted in the keynote verse of this chapter, another area that often affects well-meaning Christians is grumbling (complaining) and arguing. I am going to focus on the grumbling and complaining aspect of that verse, as it seems to impact almost every believer that I know.

Have you ever complained about your job? How about your boss? Maybe the annoying neighbor? How about the fact that you do not make enough money? Maybe the pastor's preaching is not up to snuff, or the worship music is either too loud or not loud enough. How about the slow waiter at the restaurant? If you are in school, what about that boring teacher? Hitting even closer to home, do you ever complain about your spouse or your disobedient children? Unfortunately, the list of potential complaints is endless. It wasn't hard for me to rattle off this list of potential complaints. Maybe that is because I am a little too close to them myself!

I think it is important to note where Philippians 2:14 appears in Scripture. It is right after the very notable passage of Scripture in Philippians 2:1-11 that describes the absolute humility and servanthood of Christ. Philippians 2:6-8 says, *"Who (Jesus), being in very nature God, did not consider equality with God something to be grasped, but made Himself nothing, taking the very nature of a servant, being made in human likeness. And being in appearance as a man, He humbled Himself and became obedient to death – even death on a cross."*

If there was ever anyone who had a right to grumble and complain, it was Jesus. Jesus was God, yet He had to make Himself nothing as a man and die a gruesome death on a cross so that all men might have the opportunity to live eternally with God. I think you and I might have complained if we were thrust into that situation, but what did Jesus do?

He "became obedient to death." Everywhere in the New Testament, we are implored to live as Jesus did. I have searched the New Testament and cannot find one single time when Jesus complained. Not once.

Grumbling and complaining is really a very selfish thing. When we grumble and complain, we are, in essence, telling Jesus Christ that we do not deserve the situation that we are in. We are too good for it. In reality, it is an affront to Christ Himself. He knows every situation that we are in. He has either caused it or allowed it. The real question is, will we seek to grow in our relationship to Christ because of the situation and give Him glory, or will we complain about it? I realize that what I am saying is easier said than done, but that does not mean we should lower the standard Christ has laid out for us.

Look at the next verse, Philippians 2:15. It lays out the "why" of not grumbling or complaining: *"So that you may become blameless and pure, children of God without fault in a crooked and depraved generation."* We see from this verse that the why is two-fold. First, it is so that we may further grow in our relationship with Christ, and second, it is so that Christians might be strong witnesses for the sake of Christ in this world.

When you think about it, those are the two primary purposes for the Christian to remain on this earth, instead of immediately going to heaven upon conversion. Therefore, in order to fulfill the Christian's primary purposes for living on this earth, we must not grumble and complain. It seems to me that Jesus Christ thinks that obedience in this area is absolutely key to living an effective life for Him.

So, what is the opposite of grumbling and complaining? Consider the old adage, "having an attitude of gratitude." As seen in Scripture, Colossians 3:16 tells Christians that we should have *"gratitude in your hearts."* You and I have been put on this earth with the unbelievable opportunity to enter into an eternal relationship with the God of the

Universe. Further, while we remain on this earth, if we submit to Him in obedience, He will give us something meaningful to do to positively impact others. If we take a step back and look at this big picture, shouldn't that be a cause for gratitude?

I know that there are some of you reading this book right now that are going through very difficult situations. I am not trying to minimize those situations or make you feel guilty about a present attitude you have that may fall short of what is described in this chapter. The hurt you and I sometimes feel cannot just be glossed over.

But we also cannot ignore what those who call themselves Christians are called to do. We either believe Romans 8:28, or we do not: ***"And we know that in <u>all things</u> God works for the good of those who love Him, who have been called according to His purpose."***

The alternative to embracing this verse is just not a good one. It is one of grumbling, complaining, and maybe even becoming angry at God. Let's resist the temptation to fall into the trap that we see so many around us doing and embrace the command of Philippians 2:14 and the encouragement of Romans 8:28.

CHAPTER 12

Don't Worry

Who of you by worrying can add a single hour to his life?
Matthew 6:27

I think the command not to worry may be the single most disobeyed command by Jesus in the Bible. Notice that I said "command." Jesus didn't make a suggestion for us not to worry; He commanded it. Jesus makes the command very definitively in Matthew 6:33-34:

> **"But seek first His Kingdom and His righteousness, and all these things (your needs) will be given to you as well. Therefore, do not worry about tomorrow, for tomorrow will worry about itself. Each day has enough trouble of its own."**

I will return to this passage a little later in the chapter, but let's first think about some of the sources of worry that we have. I am convinced that the medical advice sites on the Internet may be one of man's worst inventions. You know the sites. They are the ones that give just enough information to self-diagnose yourself into having cancer for almost any ailment you might have. If they were not so damaging to some people's psyches, and yes their faith, the way these sites cause people to worry might be a bit humorous.

In my family alone, I have heard of the potential for one or more members of my immediate family to be developing cancer, developing a stroke, having a heart attack, and developing Parkinson's disease. For those of you who may be experiencing any of these things, my heart goes out to you, and I am certainly not trying to demean the seriousness of your situation. But the point I am making is not about a particular disease, but about the element of worry. Although the above conditions have been self-diagnosed by my family, none of these diagnoses have actually been true! But some of my family members certainly afforded themselves the opportunity to unnecessarily worry about these things.

When you stop and think about it, there is not very much in life that we do not put under the umbrella of worry. Our jobs, relationships, family, money, politics, previously mentioned medical conditions, the potential for pain and suffering, death, and eternity. You could add just about anything in life to this list. In the chapter on *Trusting Christ in Uncertain Times*, I wrote about how I had embarrassingly worried about the twitching in my legs being a potentially life-ending neuromuscular disease. Instead, it ended up a relatively minor back issue with far less consequences.

Think about all the negative impacts of worry: high blood pressure, anxiety, depression, and the inability to perform at peak levels. Now, think about all the benefits of worry. Can you hear the crickets??? That's right; if you are like me, you probably had a really hard time coming up with even one benefit.

I still cannot think of one. But I might add a very significant negative impact — disobedience to Jesus Christ.

I am not saying that we should not be <u>concerned</u> about certain aspects of our lives. For example, we should be concerned about marrying the right person. We should be concerned about making proper career choices pleasing to God. We should be concerned about our children's well-being, spiritual development, and education. We should be concerned about our Christian witness to non-believers.

In fact, we should not just be concerned. We should also make plans related to these things so that we can be more effective in whatever we do. But there is a big difference between worry and concern. With concern, we engage Christ with us in the process, seeking Him to guide us to make good decisions and the right choices. We make a declaration that we trust Him to help us through whatever we are dealing with.

With worry, we take Christ out of the process. We are willfully disobeying His command not to worry, and we are not trusting Him to take care of us through the situation that is presenting itself in our lives. Remember, God has either caused or allowed every situation that enters our lives. There is no other choice. If we are to be obedient to Him, we must turn to Him, and not ourselves, to see us through the situation. At its core, worry is about self and not about Christ.

Sometimes, we worry about what other people will think about us — how we look, how our clothes look, or how we speak. I am not saying we should not respect other people and attempt to present ourselves in a positive manner. But worrying about what other people *think* about us may just be the worst form of worry a person can have. Christians should be most concerned about how they present themselves to Christ. Colossians 3:23 states it succinctly, ***"Whatever you do, work at it with all your heart, as <u>working for the Lord, not for men</u>."***

When my daughter Joanna ("Jo") played college basketball, like most of us would in that situation, she would worry about what the coach would think of her play. If she did not play well, she would not get more opportunities to play. When you come off the bench, you often have limited time in a game to make a positive impact for your team. Worse yet, you might make a negative impact.

Jo and I started talking about how she should play for "An Audience of One." For the Christian, you are not playing to impress the coach. You are playing for a much higher standard — you are playing to please Jesus Christ, the true "Audience of One."

It is no different in the workplace, relationships, politics, etc. The Christian "plays" for Jesus Christ, not for man. That is how we apply Colossians 3:23. We work for the Lord and not for men. When we do that, we know that He is pleased with our attempt at a pure heart and maximum effort. It is not about the results. It is about the relationship with Christ. When we focus on Christ we are no longer focused on worry. Worry is man created. It is a sin. It is not of God.

Look back at the keynote verse for this chapter, Matthew 6:27. Jesus tells us that worry will not add a single hour to your life. In fact, worry will likely shorten your life because of the various physical and emotional ailments that can result from worry. Have you ever thought to yourself, "I sure wish I would have worried more?" I can tell you that I have never thought that and I doubt you ever have either.

I have tried to make a case in this chapter that worry is a focus on self and not on Christ. Look at what Jesus said in Matthew 6:33. He tells us to *"seek first His Kingdom and His righteousness."* Jesus has, in fact, given us the anecdote for worry. The anecdote is Himself. More specifically, the anecdote is seeking Christ.

In other words, we are to be so wrapped up in seeking Him through the various situations of life that we do not have time to even think about worrying. Pursuing greater intimacy with Christ and giving Him glory should be our goal in each and every situation, not worrying about an outcome. Besides, God already knows the outcome. He knows how He is going to use it in your life to draw you closer to Him and to gain glory for Himself.

We are told in Romans 8:28, *"And we know that in all things God works for the good of those who love Him, who have been called according to His purpose."* He is not telling Christians that He will work for good in our lives in some things, or in most things, but in all things. So, analyze this a bit. What are we really worried about? We are told to seek Him and that He will work for the good of those who do. So instead of worrying, seek Him! Seek Him and trust Him for the results.

The best situation we can be in life is where we must rely on Christ and not ourselves. It is the most exciting and exhilarating place to be in life. It is also how we were designed to be all along. In John 15:5, Jesus says that He is the Vine and we are the branches and that we can do nothing apart from Him. So rather than worry about outcomes, seek to let Him be the true Vine in your life, and let him be in control of those outcomes.

In Matthew 6:34, Jesus seems to be almost facetious in His approach. He tells us that tomorrow will worry about itself. Last time I checked "tomorrow" has no capacity to worry. It seems like He is telling us just how ludicrous it is to worry; by leaving worry up to "tomorrow." He ends the verse with, ***"each day has enough trouble of its own."*** In other words, rather than worry about tomorrow, invest everything you have in what is right in front of you today. If you worry so much about tomorrow, you might just miss out on something crucial or very exciting about today.

Jesus tells us in John 16:33, ***"In this world you will have trouble. But take heart! I have overcome the world."*** Jesus Himself acknowledges that the human plight will not be perfect; there will be trouble. But once again He has given us the anecdote for dealing with the trouble, and that anecdote is Jesus Himself. The next time you are tempted to worry, turn your attention instead toward a pursuit of Christ. You may as well do that because the source of your worry was either put there or allowed there by Christ Himself, with the express purpose of drawing you closer to Him.

Christ gave us, through the apostle Paul, one of the more notable commands in Scripture, Philippians 4:6-7:

> ***"Do not be anxious about anything, but in everything, by prayer and petition, with thanksgiving, present your requests to God. And the peace of God, which transcends all understanding, will guard your hearts and your minds in Christ Jesus."***

If I could summarize this verse in my own way, I think it would be, "When trouble comes my way, seek Christ and gain peace."

One of my good friends has a specific way in which he seeks or pursues Christ when he becomes worried. You may relate to it as well.

He recognizes that the source of his worry is either or both: 1) trying to take responsibility for something that is outside his control, or 2) a lack of faith that God will not get it right (my friend's idea of right!). So, he reasons that when it comes to worrying, he needs more faith and less control. Said another way, he tries to surrender. As a practical step, he asks Christ for faith in the area where he is worried and he verbally releases the issue to Christ. He then repeats this as many times as he feels the worry coming upon him. This is just one way you may want to approach the issues causing worry in your life.

In Matthew 12:43-44 Jesus is speaking to a group of Pharisees about how a person that has had an evil spirit driven from him has to then fill his life with Himself to avoid having the evil spirit return in earnest with seven more spirits more wicked than the first evil spirit:

> *"When an evil spirit comes out of a man, it goes through arid places seeking rest and does not find it. Then it says, I will return to the house I left. When it arrives, it finds the house unoccupied, swept clean and put in order."*

Notice how Jesus describes the spirit of a person who is not pursuing Him. That person's spirit is "arid." In other words, there is nothing there. He goes on to say that the person's house is "swept clean and in order." Again, nothing there. If we do not fill our lives with an honest pursuit of Jesus Christ, we will be arid and swept clean, subject to Satan coming in, taking hold of our lives, and subjecting ourselves to worry.

This passage informs us about what we need to do about worry or any other spiritual issue in our lives. The implication here is that we must fill our lives with Christ in order to keep from having strongholds in our lives. In other words, we must be in such a consistent and constant pursuit of Christ that we simply "crowd out" worry in our lives. This is like the idea of when we are feeling down or depressed, we should minister to someone else. We should attempt to perform an act of service. Doing so serves to crowd out the depression.

It appears clear in Scripture that the real anecdote for worry is an honest, consistent, heartfelt pursuit of Christ. If you find yourself worrying more than you would like, I would encourage you to take a hard look at your spiritual disciplines. Are you daily in His Word and prayer? Is it a priority for you? Are you in fellowship with other believers on a regular basis? Are you being discipled, and/or discipling someone else? Are you engaged in regular worship? Are you serving others through the church and/or other worthwhile ministries? I think you get the point. Let's you and I fill up our lives with Christ and crowd out the worry which otherwise wants to creep in.

Look at it realistically, do you think Jesus Christ is going to give you peace, joy, and happiness in this life if you do not earnestly pursue Him? I sincerely doubt it. You were made to pursue Jesus Christ. Embrace that thought and watch Him go to work in your life.

CHAPTER 13

Forgiveness

Therefore, if you are offering your gift at the altar
and there remember that your brother has something against you,
leave your gift there in front of the altar.
First go and be reconciled to your brother;
then come and offer your gift.
Matthew 5:23-24

I t was a misunderstanding that I just could not shake. I was in a position of authority in a volunteer capacity and had regular personal access to the leader of the organization. One day, a man that I knew well accused me of influencing the leader to use some funds in a manner that he did not agree with. The funds he was referring to were in a different account from the organization that I was involved with, and I had no access to nor had ever discussed the use of those separate funds with the leader of the organization. Yet, as much as I tried to tell this man these facts, he did not believe me. Looking back on it now, I can understand why he held that viewpoint, because he just did not have access to all of the facts.

It hurt that he did not believe me, particularly since the man is a Christian. Unfortunately, my hurt turned into anger and bitterness toward the man, which was only impacting me negatively (which is always the case with bitterness). I struggled to forgive the man for his false accusation.

My attempts at reconciliation were not fruitful, and maybe not strong enough. Still, I had an obligation to forgive, even if it did not result in reconciliation. In due course, I did that, knowing that my relationship with Christ could never be what it is supposed to be without attempts at reconciliation and forgiveness. The keynote passage of this chapter made that clear to me.

Forgiveness is just not a natural reaction for human beings. For many Christians, it is a mighty struggle. But Jesus Christ places a huge emphasis on it throughout the gospels. As the keynote passage to this chapter makes clear, we cannot have a deep, abiding relationship with Christ if we have known disagreements with others for which we have not at least attempted to achieve reconciliation. And regardless of whether we achieve reconciliation, we must forgive and still love the one with whom we are in dispute.

It is so often true that forgiveness flies in the face of the emotions we feel when we have been wronged (or at least wronged in our own minds). To forgive is usually the opposite of what we are feeling. Sometimes, the pain we are feeling is just so real, or at least seems very real to us. Besides, the person we are forgiving, from an objective point of view, really does not deserve to be forgiven. We have a right to hold a grudge, based on how we have been wronged. In our minds, that person should be seeking reconciliation with us, not the other way around!

Yet, if we are listening to Christ at all, we will likely hear the whisper of the call to reconciliation in our ear. Not only are we commanded to forgive so that our relationship with Christ can be restored according to the keynote verses of this chapter, but there are also clear human benefits resulting from our forgiveness. When you think about it, we are often a prisoner to our own lack of forgiveness. We allow bitterness to take root in our lives from a lack of forgiveness, which hurt us spiritually, and maybe physically. There is thus real power in forgiveness. It can set us free from the prison we have put ourselves in. May you and I always err on the side of grace toward another and forgive, just like we would like to be treated if we had been the transgressor ourselves.

Forgiveness indeed has great beneficial power. It will clear away our bitterness and set us free to once again be in a right relationship with Christ. The prisoner of bitterness — you and me — is set free by the power of forgiveness. There is no end to the power of forgiveness, a power that is amazing and that we receive when we exercise grace toward another human being.

Jesus makes very clear the importance that He puts on relationships in His dialogue with the Pharisees in Matthew 22:34-39. In verse 36, one of the Pharisees hopes to trap Jesus in His response by asking Him which is the greatest commandment in the Law. Jesus probably chuckled to Himself at the Pharisee thinking that he could trap Him in His own words. Of course, Jesus replies in verses 37 and 38 that loving God with all your heart, soul, and mind is the first and greatest commandment. But then He quickly adds in verse 39, *"And the second is like it: Love your neighbor as yourself."* Jesus then summarizes in verse 40, *"All the Law and the Prophets hang on these two Commandments."*

Jesus groups the relationships we have with people in with the relationship we have with God. It is clear the importance Jesus places upon human relationships because they impact each Christian's individual relationship with Himself.

Matthew 18:21-35 records the Parable of the Unmerciful Servant. In this parable, the servant's master forgives a large debt of the servant because the servant begged him to do so. (Of course, this is exactly what Christ does for us when we earnestly ask Him to do so.) However, that servant then goes out and has no mercy on another person who owes him and has that person thrown in jail until he can repay his debt. The other servants of the master are troubled by this and tell their master. Upon hearing this, the master becomes angry and now has the servant thrown in jail for the debt the master originally forgave. Jesus concludes the parable by saying this in Matthew 18:35, *"This is how my heavenly Father will treat each of you unless you forgive your brother from your heart."* Note once again the importance Jesus places on human relationships. He requires us to have a forgiving spirit toward others in order to receive His forgiveness.

Going back to the beginning of the parable, Peter starts the dialogue by asking Jesus in verse 21, *"Lord, how many times shall I forgive my brother when he sins against me? Up to seven times?"* Peter says this thinking that seven times is a lot to forgive someone. Sounds like a lot to me! However, Jesus responds in verse 22 in this way, *"I tell you, not seven times, but seventy-seven times."* The implication here is that the Christian's capacity to forgive should be endless, much like our Lord and Savior's capacity to forgive all who truly seek forgiveness from Him.

So how do we overcome this strong, sometimes overwhelming feeling of resentment, anger, and bitterness when someone hurts us? It is one thing to know what God expects us to do, but how do we move from knowing in our heads to forgiving with our hearts? To love someone is to want and do what is best for them, even (and often) when it means we must make that a priority over our own feelings or desires. Even as He hung on the cross, Jesus asked the Father to forgive the very people who were crucifying Him, even though they did not ask Him for it (Luke 23:34).

In reality, the person on the other side who is creating the hurt needs more of Jesus in those moments — and the only way they may see Him is through an unsolicited offer of forgiveness from the very person or people they are hurting. This kind of forgiveness often requires us to ask God through prayer for His great love and grace to flow through our hearts to the other person.

As I close this chapter, I encourage you to think about those in your life for whom you have not sought reconciliation and for whom you have withheld forgiveness. I am thinking about it myself! It might be your spouse, one or more of your children, your Mom or Dad, your estranged friend, your neighbor, a business associate, or a friend at church or some other organization — it could be almost anyone that you have had contact with.

Some of the hurts you have experienced might be deep and seemingly unforgivable. But if we honestly look closely at every hurt, there is just not one good reason not to forgive. It is good for the other person, good for you (your health and attitude, at a minimum), and most importantly, it is good (and absolutely critical) for your relationship with Jesus Christ. I encourage you to forgive so your relationship with Christ can flourish.

CHAPTER 14

Spiritual Disciplines

I (Jesus) am the vine; you are the branches.
If a man remains in Me and I in him, he will bear much fruit;
apart from Me you can do nothing.
John 15:5

I meet regularly with several men in one-on-one discipleship relationships. The discussions most often center on how a person can get to know Christ better and come into greater intimacy with Him. **"As iron sharpens iron, so one man sharpens another"** (Proverbs 27:17).

I had one guy tell me one time that the way he could get to know Christ better was by doing good things for other people. He reasoned that if he did good things, God would honor that and draw him closer to God. Of course, guys will often talk about going to church, listening to a good sermon that they can apply in life, and participating in worship. Some guys will get in small discussion groups that they reason will help them draw closer to God.

You know, all the things I just mentioned are good. And in some ways, they will draw you closer to Christ. I would not discourage any of them. But over the years, as I have looked at my own spiritual journey, I have found that there is just no substitute for a daily quiet time with Christ.

If you are not familiar with the "quiet time" term, I define it as a daily time of reading and meditating on God's Word and talking/listening to God in a spirit of prayer.

If you are a married person, think about how you get to know your spouse better. You spend concentrated time with him or her. You communicate with your spouse on a regular basis. If you are a Christian, you hopefully spend time in prayer with your spouse. The bottom line is that you seek to develop intimacy with your spouse by spending time with them and communicating with them. Having a daily quiet time with God is no different in concept. Your goal is spiritual intimacy with the God who created you.

What a privilege God has given to us. The Creator of the Universe and of all mankind allows us to spend individual, intimate time with Him. Why should He even care about that? But He does! Knowing this, how can we not take advantage of it? When you stop and think about it, how foolish it is not to crave this kind of spiritual intimacy with Christ.

Not only is it a privilege, but He has also given us the one tool that we need to take advantage of that privilege. That tool is the Bible — the Word of God. God has given us a guidebook by which to first come to faith in Him, then learn to know Him better, and finally to learn how to live a meaningful and purposeful life. When you think about it, it seems crazy that we would do anything other than to desire to be in this Word of God every day.

Even if we look at it from a purely selfish standpoint, we will be a lot more successful in life if we would do what the Word of God says. If we followed what God's Word says, we would also avoid the many pitfalls of life that we get ourselves into.

Within the Word of God, we can read of the life and teachings of Christ. Jesus addresses nearly every major concern of life in the New

Testament. You name it — salvation, relationships, money, pride, how to work, dealing with sin, anger, selfishness, how to speak, marriage, priorities, giving, and love. These are just the things that quickly come to mind, but the significant life topics that Jesus addresses are numerous and comprehensive.

So, it is likely that if you are facing an issue in life, God has already addressed it in the Bible. And if He has not addressed your particular issue specifically, there is likely a spiritual principle that can be applied. I have heard it said that if a person lived solely by what Jesus said in the Sermon on the Mount, in Matthew chapters 5 through 7, that would be all that a person needs to live successfully. (Of course, every person should still read the entire Bible. It is just too rich not to do so.)

Look for a moment at the keynote verse of this chapter, John 15:5. In this verse, Jesus describes people as branches emanating from Him — the Vine. We all know that a branch cannot live on its own. Without the vine, all branches die. The vine provides all the nourishment the branches need to sustain life. So, it only makes sense that if a person is not connected to the One True Vine, Jesus Christ, that person can do nothing of significance in this life.

Jesus puts it rather bluntly, "you can do nothing." But, if we are connected to the Vine, Jesus tells us that we will bear much fruit. It is thus imperative that a person stays connected to the Vine so that he/she can live an effective, productive life which honors Jesus Christ. Knowing this Scriptural truth, hopefully you can see the absolute importance of a daily quiet time with the Lord.

If you are not currently having a daily quiet time with God, hopefully I have encouraged you to do so. For those of you who are daily in this most important practice, I know you see the value in it. There are a lot of ways to approach a daily quiet time and I will cover a few of those in the next paragraphs. However, no matter what the approach, the goal is always the same — to develop greater intimacy with Christ today than you had yesterday. The methods to get there can vary from person to person, but the goal is to be constant and consistent.

One of the first things to address is *when* in the day you should set aside time to have a daily quiet time. There is no right answer; a lot depends on your daily schedule. However, I must confess that I am bias to first thing in the morning before you start your daily activities. Once your day begins, a myriad of interruptions can take place, not to mention the known tasks you need to accomplish each day. As a result, you may find it difficult to get a quiet time alone with Christ once the day has begun in earnest.

But, if you start the day with a quiet time, it is much easier to get alone, not be interrupted, and spend concentrated time with the Lord. Plus, what a fabulous way to get the day off to a great start. You can start your day with an intake of God's Word to set the tone for your day.

I have had several friends, and fellow Christians, tell me that they simply do not have the time to set aside for a daily quiet time. I have two responses to that. First, you cannot afford not to take the time. Think of all that you will lose if you do not take the time, including greater intimacy with Christ, peace and contentment, direction in life, spiritual confidence to face life challenges, etc. Second, if you think you do not have the time, just get up 15 minutes earlier. I promise you that you will feel more energized by having a quiet time vs. getting 15 more minutes of sleep.

Which brings up the topic of the *length* of quiet time. I just mentioned 15 minutes and I think that is a good place to start. If you are new to developing this practice, that is probably a reasonable goal. However, depending on the content of your quiet time, you may find that 15 minutes is not enough.

I know Christians who spend anywhere from 15 minutes to two hours per day; and in some cases, more than two hours. But do not make it so much about the length of the time. Rather, make it about what is necessary for you to develop the depth of the relationship with Christ you are seeking with Him and He is seeking with you.

We are now ready to talk about *content*. As I mentioned before, this can vary widely from person to person. Below are a few suggestions based on what I have done in my 43 years as a Christian and what I have observed others doing:

- Read through one book of the Bible, possibly covering about one chapter per day. Keep a journal of what you learned and pray about how you can apply what you learned to your daily life.

- Read the Bible through in a year. There are many plans that you can incorporate to aid you in doing that. Because of the volume of reading that this requires, the caution here is that you may not be able to spend a great deal of time journaling and meditating on what you read. Still, every Christian should read the Bible cover-to-cover at some point in their life, if not multiple times.

- Use a Bible study aid such as a Navigator study or devotional. These studies can walk you through books of the Bible and/or specific passages of Scripture and ask you questions that help you better understand what you have read and guide you to finding application to your daily living.

These are just a few suggestions for developing your content. Other spiritual disciplines that should accompany your personal study of Scripture are as follows:

- Keep a journal to record new learnings, inspirations, and prayer requests and how those requests were answered. I mentioned in the chapter on *Becoming a Patriarch or Matriarch* that the way that I journal is by writing a note to my wife, children, and sons-in-law every day on what I learned in my Bible reading for the day. This helps me to understand better what I read since I now must write about it to others. It also allows me to impart God's Word to those I love most and to set an example for having a daily quiet time. At a minimum, even if you do not keep a journal, make sure you are monitoring how Christ is working in your life as a result of prayer.

- Memorize Scripture, usually by taking a personally relevant verse from what you read in your quiet time. Unfortunately, I find that this is a practice that is not very common among most Christians. In Jeremiah 31:33, God says, *"I will put My law in their minds and write it on their hearts."* When we memorize Scripture, it becomes a part of who we are. It is available to us for ready recall to face the challenges of life. Memorizing Scripture should be a practice for every serious Christian.

Before leaving the topic of daily quiet time, I want to emphasize that once you have completed your daily focused time with God that does not mean you do not still stay engaged with Him throughout the day. First Thessalonians 5:17 tells us to *"pray continually."* Obviously, we cannot have a focused time of prayer 24 hours of the day. Most of us have daily activities such as work, care for children, volunteering, etc.

However, we are never to lose our communion with Christ throughout the day. We are to stay in a spirit of prayer, if not in actual prayer. There may be times during the day where we can have focused prayer, but for many of us most of our efforts will be to stay in a spirit of prayer. In summary, our quiet time does not end our time with Christ for the day.

One other comment about prayer. Every believer should have concentrated prayer daily. But in addition to that, I would encourage every believer to build into their schedule regular times of extended prayer. That may happen once a week for some, or a little more frequently or a little less frequently for others. But extended times of prayer are important for developing a deep, intimate relationship with Christ.

I am not saying that the length of your prayers determines their quality. But what I am saying is that if we really want to develop a strong, intimate relationship with Christ, we will spend extended time with Him on regular occasions, just as Jesus was in the practice of doing with the Father.

In fact, Jesus modeled this extended time of prayer for us. Matthew 14:23-25 records an extended time of prayer for Jesus, right after he had fed the five thousand and right before he walked on the water out to a boat the disciples (including Peter) were in.

Matthew 14:25 says that Jesus walked on the water toward the disciples' boat during the "fourth watch" of the night. According to Roman tradition, that was 3:00 AM – 6:00 AM. But before that, verse 23 records, *"After He had dismissed them (the five thousand), He went up on the mountainside by Himself to pray. When evening came, He was there alone."*

So, Jesus had gone to pray sometime in the afternoon because the evening had not yet come. He then was not seen walking on the water until no earlier than 3:00 AM. The implication here is that Jesus probably prayed for 10-12 hours. As you can see, Jesus undoubtedly engaged with the Father in extended times of prayer.

I have focused most of this chapter on developing a daily quiet time for the purpose of growing in intimacy with Christ as the core of how a person develops spiritually as a believer. But there are still other important disciplines that I believe every Christian should be engaged in. Church attendance in a Bible-believing, Christ-preaching church is important as it does several things for the believer; including intake of God's Word through regular teaching and preaching, corporate worship, fellowship, and calls to service and giving.

It is also a place to become involved in both in-reach to believers and outreach to non-believers. Many churches value missions, which are a great way to grow in Christ and impact others for Christ by participating in mission work, both in this country and abroad. Hebrews 10:24-25 tells believers, *"And let us consider how we may spur one another on toward love and good deeds. Let us not give up meeting together, as some are in the habit of doing, but let us encourage one another — and all the more as you see the Day approaching."*

Christians have been called to meet from the very beginning of Christianity. We need to meet to spur each other on toward love and good deeds and to encourage each other. Churches are a natural place to do that.

On a more intimate level, many churches encourage that people gather together in small groups. This provides a greater level of accountability and shrinks the corporate church experience to one where we can encourage and hold each other accountable in more specific ways. This brings the call of Hebrews 10:24-25 down to a greater level of intimacy and accountability. It is also a place where the small group can get very specific about ministry opportunities to the non-believing world. These kinds of opportunities may not be limited to just the church. There are plenty of Christian ministries that may foster this kind of fellowship and accountability experience as well.

A still further greater level of intimacy is one-on-one accountability with another believer. The Bible affirms that Jesus will be right in the midst of this one-on-one gathering of believers when Jesus says in Matthew 18:20, *"For where two or three come together in My name, there I am with them."*

Oftentimes, these one-on-one meetings take the form of Christian discipleship, in a Paul/Timothy type of relationship modeled in the Bible, where Paul acted as Timothy's spiritual mentor. They could also take the form of accountability partners or be a combination of both types of these relationships.

Either way, each person has the opportunity in these kinds of relationships to confidentially share their struggles and successes and to dig in and help each other grow in intimacy with Christ. I believe this type of relationship is extremely important for a person to grow in intimacy with Christ, and I would certainly encourage it for every believer.

Of course, there are many kinds of ministries outside the formal church for a believer to invest in, both for his/her sake and for that of others. Every believer should carefully consider where they will invest their time and seek Christ to lead them in making such decisions. A believer should become involved because they are being led by the Holy Spirit in order to grow in their faith and positively impact others for the sake of Christ.

As a final thought, there will be times of "spiritual dryness" in your life. Even for the most devoted Christ-followers, there are days when you may feel weary and you really do not want to spend that daily time with Christ. This is where a heart set on Christ comes in (see Colossians 3:2) and you exercise obedience. Even when you do not feel like it, do it anyway.

You will likely find that you are very glad that you did, and your spiritual dryness will eventually dissipate. Think about it — spiritual dryness is not going to be cured by running from God's Word. On the contrary, it is at those times where we most need to lean into God's Word.

CHAPTER 15

Giving

*Each man should give
what he has decided in his heart to give,
not reluctantly or under compulsion,
for God loves a cheerful giver.*
2 Corinthians 9:7

There may not be a more tangible way to express one's faith than through giving. Giving requires a level of obedience that can sometimes "hurt." When a person gives to the cause of Christ, they are willingly making a statement of priorities. The giver is saying that the money they could have spent on something else needs to be spent on the cause of Christ, not on themselves. Giving of financial resources is similar in sacrifice to giving of our time. In both ways, a person says no to self and yes to Christ and others.

You have probably heard it said before that if you want to know a person's priorities, just look at their checkbook. You might want to try that yourself over about a three-month period, if nothing more than to see where you are spending your money. If you are a Christian, look to see how much of it goes to your local church and to other charities that advance the gospel of Jesus Christ. Hopefully, you will find that you have placed Christ high on your list of priorities (of course, He should be first) and that is evidenced by how you are spending your money.

So, maybe we should start to explore this topic by asking how much of your money is, in fact, your money. I suppose from a human viewpoint we could say that any money that we have earned through working or investing is our money. But from God's point of view — from a spiritual perspective, we might also conclude that none of it is our money — it all belongs to God. He gave us life and He has given us whatever talents we have to earn money. As a result, he is the genesis behind our earning power. Following that to a logical conclusion, it all belongs to Him.

Another way to think about this is the concept of ownership versus stewardship. Ownership is an attitude of controlling what we have to accomplish personal priorities and objectives. Stewardship is an attitude of managing what has been entrusted to us in order to accomplish the objectives of the true owner, who is God.

Even though it all belongs to Him, God has seemingly let us off the hook in the Old Testament when it comes to money. The Old Testament standard for giving was to tithe what you earn — giving ten percent to God. Wow. He seems to have permitted us to keep 90 percent for ourselves! If you think about it, that appears almost too good to be true for the faithful person, particularly when you consider that it all belongs to God. Yet, even the serious believer in Jesus Christ often struggles to get up to that ten percent level.

When I first started working, my wife and I started meeting with a group of young Christian couples from my work. We were all working hard, having just started in our careers, and money was very tight for all of us. At the time, Cindy and I owned a home and we had just had our first child. I was making a grand total of $16,000 per year, and we were a one-income family, as we both agreed that Cindy would be a stay at home mom for the benefit of our son at the time, and our future children.

At one of these gatherings, the topic of tithing had come up. For me, and many in the group, that was a challenging topic. Trying to make the concept a little more bearable, one of the couples asked the question of the group, "Should we tithe on the net or the gross?" I mean, it did not seem right to tithe on money that was already earmarked for the government. But I will never forget what one of the more mature guys in the group said, "Do you want to be blessed on the gross or on the net?"

There is nothing in the Bible that addresses tithing as it relates to gross or net income. Still, the point was made in my heart. I knew I wanted the blessings on my family and me to be larger, not smaller. From that point forward, Cindy and I determined that we would tithe on the gross, not the net.

This idea is definitely consistent with what the apostle Paul says in 2 Corinthians 9:6:

> *"Remember this, whoever sows sparingly will also reap sparingly, and whoever sows generously will also reap generously."*

Paul wasn't speaking about tithing here, but rather the condition of a person's heart toward giving. Still, at least for me at the time, I knew that sowing generously was the path I should attempt to go down. I will cover the concept of generous giving that Paul was referring to later in the chapter.

The concept of the tithe dates all the way back, biblically, to the time of Abram (later to be called Abraham). After Abram defeated the group of kings who had captured his nephew Lot, Abraham met with Melchizedek, king of Salem and, as recorded in Genesis 14:20, gave him a tenth of what he had as a show of gratitude to God for what God had done for him. Years later, as recorded in Genesis 28:22, his grandson Jacob, after having had an encounter with God in a dream at Bethel, pledged to God, *"of all that you give me I will give you a tenth."*

In the last book of the Old Testament, ascribed to the prophet Malachi, God tells us to test Him in the area of the tithe. Malachi 3:10 records God saying this:

> *"Bring the whole tithe into the storehouse, that there may be food in my house. Test me in this, says the Lord Almighty, and see if I will not throw open the floodgates of heaven and pour out so much blessing that you will not have room enough for it."*

The "storehouse" is commonly thought of as the local church in modern-day Christianity. There is nothing wrong with that interpretation. At a minimum, I would argue that the storehouse is any Christian ministry which advances the gospel of Jesus Christ. That happens to be most often defined today as the local church.

The Pastor of Woodlands Church in The Woodlands, TX, Kerry Shook, tells his congregation another important aspect of giving a tithe. He tells believers in the church to "pay God first." In other words, when you get paid, write out the check (or pay electronically) to your local church first. Do not wait to see if you have enough money at the end of your pay cycle to tithe. This is yet another way that we set priorities in the area of giving, making sure that the Lord is placed first in our lives.

It is also important to mention that we should never look at our giving as supporting the church budget or helping to pay the Pastor's salary. In reality, that should be the furthest thing from our minds. Giving is an act of obedience and gratitude for what Christ has done in the Christian's life. It is a way for us to tangibly acknowledge and be thankful for His active presence in our life. It is not to help to pay for anything. Sure, your giving will pay the bills of the church and support ministries. But that is not <u>why</u> you give.

So far, I have written about only the Old Testament concept, and command, to tithe. But what does the New Testament say about giving? If you think tithing was tough, let's now dive into what the New Testament further reveals to us about giving. That standard is not near as quantitative but seems to reveal an even more challenging concept. The New Testament standard requires us to seek the Lord and determine what He wants us to do. It may even require more sacrifice than tithing!

In general, I would characterize the New Testament standard of giving as "cheerful, generous giving." Look at the keynote verse for this chapter, 2 Corinthians 9:7:

> *"Each man should give what he has decided in his heart to give, not reluctantly or under compulsion, <u>for God loves a cheerful giver</u>."*

What we "decide in our heart," as written in this verse, depends on the depth and seriousness of our relationship to Jesus Christ. This verse tells us that we should give, and give cheerfully, not because we must, or are supposed to, but because we want to. We want to because of what Christ has done in our lives.

Look what Paul says about the Macedonians churches in the preceding chapter — 2 Corinthians 8:3-4:

> *"For I testify that they gave as much as they were able, and even beyond their ability. Entirely on their own, <u>they urgently pleaded with us for the privilege</u> of sharing in this service to the saints."*

The people of the Macedonian churches wanted to give! It was a high privilege because they were able to give in gratitude for how Christ had worked in their lives. The clear implication here is that they gave generously. That is the kind of giving commanded in the New Testament. It takes the discussion beyond a mere quantitative measure and now puts it into the realm of the depth of our relationship with Christ.

One caution here. I am not saying that the New Testament necessarily takes you beyond the tithe. I suppose it is possible that after seeking the Lord's guidance for the level at which you should give, you could conceivably conclude that it would be less than a tithe. However, I think it highly unlikely that is where the Lord would take the serious believer in their thinking about giving, particularly since it would contradict what He already said in Scripture about tithing. For me, I have always thought of the tithe as the "floor" for giving, with the New Testament stance of cheerful, generous giving likely taking me beyond the tithe. But every believer must decide that for themselves, led by the Holy Spirit.

The concept of sacrificial giving is also mentioned in the New Testament. Luke 21:1-4 records Jesus telling this to His disciples, within earshot of the crowd around Him:

> *"As He looked up, Jesus saw the rich putting their gifts into the temple treasury. He also saw a poor widow put in two very small copper coins. I tell you the truth, He said, this poor widow has put in more than all the others. All these people gave their gifts out of their wealth; but she out of her poverty put in all she had to live on."*

This widow gave in extreme faith, out of obedience and sacrificially. Jesus deemed her gift of much greater value than the much larger gifts of the rich, which once again brings up this extremely important point about giving. Giving is not about the amount, but about the depth of the relationship with Christ. As I discussed earlier in the chapter, giving is a tangible expression of faith. It is not about the amount and where the money will be used. It is about the Christian having the high privilege (see 2 Corinthians 8:4) of telling Jesus Christ "thank you" for saving you and living within you in this life.

One other New Testament point about giving. It is to be done in secret. Jesus tells us this about giving as part of the Sermon on the Mount in Matthew 6:3-4:

> *"But when you give to the needy, do not let your left hand know what your right hand is doing, so that your giving may be in secret. Then your Father, who sees what is done in secret, will reward you."*

Jesus started this section of the Sermon on the Mount in Matthew 6:1 by saying:

> *"Be careful not to do your acts of righteousness before men, to be seen by them. If you do, you will have no reward from your Father in heaven."*

Jesus Christ is not looking for a person to pound their chest and become prideful about their giving. In fact, as these verses articulate, He is looking for just the opposite. And if we want to become prideful about giving and let others know what we are doing, we are promised one thing — there will be no reward from God because of our own perceived outstanding level of giving.

Before I close this chapter, I want to take a moment and look at a sprinkling of Scripture related to giving, and maybe tie the Old and New Testament concepts of giving back together.

Proverbs 21:26: *"All day long he (the sluggard) craves for more, <u>but the righteous give without sparing</u>."*

Luke 6:38a (Jesus Speaking): *"Give and it will be given to you…"*

Psalm 112:5a: *"Good will come to him who is generous…"*

2 Corinthians 8:7: *"But just as you excel in everything, in faith, in speech, in knowledge, in complete earnestness and in your love for us, <u>see that you also excel in this grace of giving</u>."*

Proverbs 11:25: *"<u>A generous man will prosper;</u> he who refreshes others will himself be refreshed."*

I purposely alternated these verses between the Old and New Testament to make it clear that the directives given to us in God's Word are consistent throughout His Word. While the Old Testament has a great deal to say about tithing, it also has a great deal to say about generous giving, consistent with the New Testament commands on giving.

One final thought on giving. Thinking back to Jonah when he was in the belly of the great fish, Jonah proclaimed this to God in Jonah 2:8:

> *"Those who cling to worthless idols forfeit the grace that could be theirs."*

I am sure you have heard the adages "you can't take it with you" and "no one ever saw a hearse pulling a trailer with all of a man's stuff." *Worthless idols* can often be the money that we are so desperately holding onto for retirement, security, or some other undescribed reason.

But if we hold onto our money too tightly, we might just forfeit the grace that we could have received from Christ if we had been a generous, cheerful giver. Let us not forfeit that grace and instead allow Jesus Christ to exercise His grace over us and empower us to be that generous, cheerful giver.

CHAPTER 16

Unity Among Believers

I in them and You in Me.
May they be brought to complete unity
to let the world know that You sent Me
and have loved them even as You have loved Me.
John 17:23

"The music is too loud in that church."

"I don't like the Pastor's preaching style."

"That church is too charismatic for me."

"I can not go to a church because none of them have discipleship ministries."

"A home church is the only way to develop deep relationships among believers."

"All churches should have a Sunday School, Home Groups are not enough."

These are just a few examples of some things I have heard over the years from fellow Christians that, let's just say, "do not inspire unity."

When you pull back the covers of disunity among believers, most of the lack of unity stems from personal opinions and styles, things that are truly disputable, or discretionary matters and not essential Christian doctrinal issues.

There is often little true substance behind the issues Christians create among themselves. I have definite preferences for how I like to worship, the preaching style I like to listen to, the type of youth and children's programs in a church, the degree of emphasis on missions, etc. But the fact of the matter is that most of what I just mentioned is based on what I just said — my own personal preferences. There is no biblical basis for any disagreement with others' personal preferences in the areas I just mentioned.

Unity is not a word that many modern-day Christians like to focus on. It sounds a little too *kumbaya* for a lot of us. We reason that it may require too much compromise beyond what we are comfortable with. In today's society, we honor those who have strong opinions and know what they value. In the political world, we are encouraged to be either on the right or on the left. There is little room for compromise. Our political leaders all vote the same way depending on their political party. They are often afraid to "reach across the aisle" for fear of losing their political base. They have forgotten that we are all really on the same team — the American team.

Maybe this trend in society is influencing the body of Christ. I am not really sure. But I know this — many Christians do not value unity within the body of Christ to the degree that we should. But Jesus took unity very seriously. The keynote verse for this chapter is John 17:23. Jesus is praying to the Father the night before His crucifixion about the topic of unity among His disciples when He says the following: ***"I in them and You in Me. May they be brought to complete unity to let the world know that You sent Me and have loved them even as You have loved Me."***

Jesus tells us plainly in this verse why unity among the believers is so important: ***"To let the world know that you sent Me."*** It could not be much clearer. Simply put, a lack of unity among Christ-followers is a poor witness to the non-believing world.

Think about it. If you were ever involved in team sports, did you prefer being on a team without dissension, or did you prefer a locker room in turmoil? Frequently, the teams that are unified, but less talented, will beat the teams more talented but with dissension in the locker room. This is just one example, but it applies to nearly every area of life. If you are part of a group at work, socially, or otherwise, that is unified, you will invariably be more successful. You do not always have to think exactly like each other, but you at least need to be unified around the basic purpose or goal. Different perspectives are helpful, but all within the umbrella of wanting a successful team.

Jesus prayed the prayer in John 17:23 because He knew that the spreading of the gospel absolutely depended on it. It was a life or death situation for the proliferation of Christianity. There was no Plan B. God had chosen to use men and women who believed in Christ to tell others about their experiences so that the gospel would be available to all mankind. Jesus knew that unity was necessary for the disciples to get the job done. The opportunity for salvation for everyone who would ever live hung in the balance. The disciples had to be unified in purpose.

Of course, the gospel cannot be compromised at the altar of unity, nor can clear-cut commands given in Scripture. The basic doctrines of any God-honoring church, or body of believers, cannot be compromised. The gospel must be preached. Belief in Jesus Christ as the only way to be reconciled to God (John 14:6) is absolute. Jesus is fully God and fully man. And the Bible is the infallible Word of God.

But the form of worship, whether you have a choir, or you don't, whether you have Sunday School or Home Groups (or both), the architecture of the building you worship in, just to name a few, should not be issues that lead to a lack of unity. They are matters of personal preference, not differences in Biblical doctrine.

Instead, what some Christians end up arguing about are the "methods" used by a church, not the substance of the gospel of Jesus Christ. I have noted in recent years that it has become fashionable among some Christians to voice a degree of disdain for the "big-box seeker" churches. These are the churches that often do creative things to bring non-believers in the door, that have preaching seemingly more directed at the non-believer than the believer (the argument is that the sermons are not "meaty" enough for more mature Christians), that focus on Home Groups rather than Sunday School, that meet in buildings with more modern architecture rather than stained glass windows, etc.

The argument is that the Word of God has been watered-down, the preaching does not focus enough on the sin of man, and that these churches have been secularized into modern-day culture rather than staying true to Jesus Christ and sound biblical doctrine.

I will confess that I have been attending a "big-box seeker" church for the last 20+ years so I may be a bit biased in my thinking. If any of the things just described defined the church I go to (watered-down gospel, no discussion of sin, etc.), I can assure you that I would not go there anymore. I do not agree with every method my church has ever employed (by the way, I must also recognize that whether I agree to it or not does not make it right or wrong). But they are just methods; not a matter of substance to the gospel of Jesus Christ.

Here is what I can tell you that I have seen in the church I attend. I have seen over and over again lives transformed by the power of Jesus Christ.

That is a result I will never argue with. Does it really matter the method that was used to achieve that kind of ultimate result?

I have friends who go to churches with Sunday School, where the preaching is expositional, there is a wonderful choir, where the building has stained glass windows, and the pews are meticulously maintained. Do you know what I say about that? Fantastic! They have found a place where they are most comfortable in worshipping Christ and fellowshipping with like-minded believers.

I have far more in common with them than I have differences with them. And, what I have in common with them is far more important than what I might not have in common with them. We both believe that the Bible is the infallible Word of God, that Jesus Christ was crucified, dead, and resurrected; that every man and woman has a sin problem; and that belief in Jesus Christ is the only means to salvation. Those are the things we must rally around, not the petty differences in form and methods.

Also, churches must never compete against each other, but should always celebrate each other's successes. The goal is not the success of each individual church, but the overall advancement of the gospel to the non-believing world and the building up of the body of believers.

So far, I have written in this chapter mostly about the lack of unity among traditional and non-traditional church groups. But there is another group of well-meaning Christians to address. It is those true believers who choose not to attend any church.

Often, these are Christians who have found a particular ministry that they have devoted their lives to, choosing not to make the traditional and non-traditional forms of church a significant part of the exercise of their faith. Just like traditional and non-traditional churches should not criticize each other over disputable matters, I see no need to criticize this group of Christians as well.

For example, I know many men like this who have committed their lives to the ministry of evangelism and discipleship. They have produced a tremendous amount of fruit for the sake of Christ. How could I possibly argue with that?

I am involved in this ministry outside the church in Houston, but also choose to fully participate in a local church. I am more comfortable with that approach as I think it promotes greater unity among believers, but it is something I do not need to be dogmatic about. In essence, these group of men and their families have formed their own church — a local body of believers that is part of the greater body of Christ.

My premise, based on John 17:23, is that unity among believers is essential for the gospel to be spread to the non-believing world. Consistent with this premise is what the apostle Paul says about unity in Romans 15:5-6: *"May the God who gives endurance and encouragement give you a spirit of unity among yourselves as you follow Christ Jesus, so that with <u>one heart and mouth</u> you may glorify the God and Father of our Lord Jesus Christ."*

Not only is unity essential for the believing world to reach the non-believing world, but unity among believers is also a profound way to glorify God. Being of "one heart and mouth" gives glory to God.

CHAPTER 17

Obedience vs. Passion

Your attitude should be the same as Christ Jesus;
Who, being in very nature God,
did not consider equality with God
something to be grasped,
but made Himself nothing,
taking the very nature of a servant,
being made in human likeness.
And being found in appearance as a man,
He humbled Himself
and became obedient to death —
even death on a cross.
Philippians 2:5-8

I think Joseph, the earthly father of Jesus, is a lot like Rodney Dangerfield. He does not get any respect. He does not make the Hall of Faith in Hebrews chapter 11. But clearly he exhibited complete obedience to God's call on several occasions.

Matthew 1:24 describes what Joseph did when he awakened from a dream where an angel of the Lord had told him to continue with the plan of making Mary his wife. Even though she was pregnant without them having had sexual relations, and that the child was conceived by the Holy Spirit, the verse says, "***When Joseph woke up, <u>he did what</u>***

the angel of the Lord had commanded him *and took Mary home as his wife."*

Think about that for a minute. Joseph was not put in the best of positions. Matthew 1:19 says that Joseph was a righteous man and had decided to end their relationship when he found out Mary was pregnant, not wanting to subject her to public disgrace. But here he was being told in a dream that Mary was made pregnant by the Holy Spirit and that he should stick with her.

This whole situation was certainly not what Joseph had in mind. He was now in an embarrassing situation that would be very difficult to explain to anyone. Yet, what does he do? He wakes up from the dream and immediately does what God called him to do, with not a clue as to what lay ahead.

Do you think that was what Joseph wanted to do from a human perspective? Do you think he had any "passion" around that decision? The dictionary defines passion as "an intense desire or enthusiasm for something." Another definition might go something like this, "an intense, driven conviction to pursue something that motivates or inspires." I will bet Joseph had nothing of the sort for this path he was given; yet, he chose obedience over passion.

Deciding to keep Mary to be his wife would turn out to be just one of Joseph's decisions that required obedience and faith (and without passion). In Matthew 2:13, an angel of the Lord again appears to Joseph, this time telling him to take Jesus and Mary into Egypt. No further details are given – just go. Matthew 2:14 tells us what Joseph did in response to the Lord, *"So he got up, took the child and his mother during the night and left for Egypt."*

No hesitation. No sleeping on it for another night or thinking about it longer. He did not even pray over it for several days, as Christians sometimes like to do. He simply was obedient to God's call to do something he likely did not want to do and had no idea about the length of time or outcome.

Joseph again displayed his obedience when an angel of the Lord appeared to him in another dream after Herod died, telling him to now return to Israel. By now, I am sure you are not surprised by what Joseph did. In Matthew 2:21, Joseph displayed his instant obedience yet again, ***"So he got up, took the child and His mother and went to the land of Israel."***

In each of the three instances just described, I am sure Joseph had doubts, fears, and a lot of uncertainty. Yet he was obedient to what God called him to do. But even beyond the uncertainty, doubts, and fear, I am certain that Joseph had very little "passion" for what he was being called to do. He just did it, even though he lacked the passion that all of us like to have when we embark upon something big in our lives.

In both the Christian and non-Christian worlds, we are encouraged to find our passion in life and pursue it, even to the point where we might be able to make a living exercising our passion. I cannot really argue with the premise. It makes sense that each of us will be better wherever we possess passion. But we cannot live our lives pursuing only those things for which we have a passion. Sometimes, we are called simply to be obedient, including filling the gap for a hole that exists, at least temporarily.

Maybe nowhere will this be more prevalent than in the life of a church. How about helping in the nursery, or leading a Home Group or Sunday School class, or serving as an elder or deacon, or serving on the Budget Committee? I am sure you have a few you could add to the list. What we must remember is that sometimes God calls us to merely serve, even if we have no passion for the service. We do not always know why, though it may one day be revealed to us. But one thing is for sure, when we choose obedience over passion, the choice to do so requires humility and self-sacrifice. We have a great model to follow for this — Jesus Christ Himself.

Philippians 2:5-8, the keynote verses of this chapter, records the model for being obedient when we would rather choose another path that appears more interesting and exciting. What did Jesus do, according to Philippians 2:5-8? He humbled Himself, became a servant to mankind, and became obedient to His sacrificial death on the cross.

The obedience we are called to is nothing compared to this. Luke 22:42 records Jesus praying this the night before He was crucified, *"Father, if You are willing, take this cup from Me; yet not my will, but Yours be done."* As we know, God's plan was that Jesus fulfill the sacrifice for mankind once and for all. As a result, Jesus proceeded willingly, so that every person who has or ever will live will have the opportunity to gain eternal life.

Almost a year ago, I felt like Cindy and I were being called by God to lead a Home Group in our church. I did not have any particular passion around it. I was already in a men's group that meets every two weeks for accountability and encouragement, and in another men's group in our church that meets for prayer every week. Personally, I did not feel a need to be involved in another group. But the church had a need for leaders of these groups, so Cindy and I volunteered to do it.

It has turned out to be a great blessing, as we have made a new group of friends who are serious about their faith, for whom we enjoy being around, and for whom we can collectively engage in ministry to others. In addition, it has given Cindy and me an opportunity to be in fellowship together with believers, and not just me doing my own thing. Like I just described, do not be surprised if God blesses you for your obedience. You may begin to enjoy whatever you reluctantly volunteer for. And yes, one day you may just develop a passion for it as well.

Admittedly, I am not a very "artsy" guy. I have no passion for the arts. I will always choose a good sporting event over the arts. However, a few years back, I began attending plays, both in New York and in Houston. While I will still choose a football game over Broadway, my eyes have been opened to experiencing other parts of life that can bring joy. Sometimes, this too will be the result of your obedience over passion. You may not fully embrace whatever you were obedient to, but you will gain a greater appreciation for the activity.

The Bible is full of people and events who chose obedience in uncertain situations over passion. The patriarchs of the faith like Abraham, Jacob, Joseph, Moses, and David, just to name a few, all did things they were uncomfortable with but were nonetheless told to do. I like the way Hebrews 11:8 says how Abraham responded when he was told to enter the Promised Land: he *"obeyed and went, even though he did not know where he was going."* That may well be the definition of obedience over passion.

Sometimes, faithfulness and obedience will call us to be like Abraham — to go where we do not know where we are going. To go to places for which we know we have no initial passion to proceed. Yet, when we step out of our comfort zone and obediently step into a situation where we have no passion, it is then that we know that we have gained some measure of spiritual maturity, hopefully making us more pleasing to God.

In closing, I am certainly not trying to discourage Christians from seeking to become involved in places where they have God-given passions. On the contrary, as I previously mentioned, we will likely be more effective in areas where we have the greatest God-given passions. But in understanding this, I encourage you not to discount the fact that God may call you to work in areas outside your passions. And if you hear a clear call to do so from Christ, choose obedience over passion.

CHAPTER 18

Big Faith

Which of you, if his son asks for bread, will give him a stone?
Of if he asks for a fish, will give him a snake?
If you, then, though you are evil,
know how to give good gifts to your children,
how much more will your Father in heaven
give good gifts to those who ask Him!
Matthew 7:9-11

It happened about ten years ago, but I remember it like it was yesterday. It was the realization that our youngest daughter's torn anterior cruciate ligament (ACL) had been miraculously healed. Let me start this story by giving you a little background on our youngest of four children, Joanna.

Joanna (Jo) was a college basketball player at Abilene Christian University (ACU) in Abilene, TX. She had been a very good high school player and received a full athletic scholarship to play at ACU. Two days before she was to start her senior year at The Woodlands High School in The Woodlands, TX, she went up for a breakaway lay-up in a scrimmage game. An opposing player bumped her in mid-air and she came down awkwardly on her right knee.

137

My wife, Cindy, and I were in the stands. We both thought she would just shake it off, get up, and continue playing, as she had done so many times in the past. But we quickly learned that this time was going to be different. She was not getting up quickly and Jo knew that her injury was serious. Still, her mother and I hoped for the best. We had seen other girls lose a season to an ACL injury, and we were hopeful that in a season where this would be "her team" to lead, that she would still be able to play.

Cindy, Jo, and I immediately prayed for Jo to be okay, or if she was not okay, for her to be healed quickly. The next day she got an MRI and the results came back — a torn ACL. It was a devastating blow for Jo, and frankly, for Cindy and me. The year before she had been a starter at point guard, distributing the ball to some talented teammates. For her senior year, she had been moved to shooting guard to better utilize her talents. The year was set up nicely for her to be in a position for her personal success, as well as the success of the team, but it was not to be for Jo (though the team did make it to the playoffs that year).

That was a hard year for sports in the Harner household. Our son, Josh (our oldest), had played college basketball and had a very nice career. We had another daughter, Jaymie, who also played a year of college ball and who was a very good high school player on a very good team. All-in-all, while our kids had experienced ups and downs in sports, they had been largely successful, which had provided a great deal of enjoyment for Cindy and me. But now we dutifully went to every game and watched as the other girls and families experienced what we had hoped to experience. It was hard, but it wasn't impossible. I know Cindy and I leaned into Christ a little harder that year, as did Jo, and our faith grew.

Fortunately, ACU's coach thought enough of Jo to still honor her scholarship. So, while she missed her entire senior year in high school, she would have another chance to play in college. Jo had surgery shortly after her injury to replace her ACL with a piece of her patella tendon so that she would be ready to play her freshman year at ACU.

Jo arrived on the ACU campus in August the next year for her freshman year and was doing fairly well in pre-season drills. However, in a pre-season intra-squad scrimmage, her knee again gave out, though this time it was only a partial ACL tear. She tried to brace it up and continue to play, but she soon learned that she was not going to be able to continue to do so. That Thanksgiving she had her second ACL surgery, this time using a cadaver ACL.

If her high school senior year was a bad year for the Harner household, this year was even worse. I know Jo would tell you that she was bitter, to some degree, about the whole situation. Her faith was tested, though it never broke. She seriously contemplated quitting basketball and was headed down that path for much of her freshman year right into the summer between her freshman and sophomore years. If the truth would be told, Cindy and I probably preferred that she continue to play because we wanted her to realize her potential. It just seemed like such a "downer" way for her to finish playing.

However, we also knew that she would have to want to play, and we certainly did not want her to do something she was not "all-in" to do. In addition, she actually had not been too thrilled about her freshman year in general. She never felt completely comfortable at ACU, maybe because of her somewhat depressed feelings about her inability to play. She had met a young man there on the ACU football team by the name of Casey Carr near the end of her freshman year, but the relationship had barely started, so that was not enough to bring her back to ACU either.

Near the end of that summer between her freshman and sophomore years, Jo told us that she had been praying and seeking God in the decision. She had decided to continue to play, feeling comfortable that was the direction God was leading her to follow. Cindy and I were somewhat surprised, but she seemed very confident that she had heard from the Lord. We endorsed her decision and felt like God was going to do great things through her. In our minds we thought those "great things" would primarily be realized on the basketball court. However, as I am about to tell you, our plans and God's plans were going to be a bit different, as they often are.

For the next two years, Jo saw limited action on the basketball court. As I look back on it, being a former college player myself, I now realize Jo was working those two years just to regain the athleticism that she had back in high school, let alone regain and improve upon her basketball talent. Still, because we wanted to support Jo to realize her potential on the court, Cindy and I would often travel six hours to see her play in a game, sometimes for just a minute or two, or even not at all. We would do this not just for weekend games but for mid-week games as well, even though I was still working full-time at a very busy job.

We wanted her to know that we stood behind her and supported her in her goal to be a strong contributor to the team. Even though Jo was not experiencing the amount of playing time we all hoped for, the relationship with Casey that had just barely begun at the end of her freshman year was beginning to become more serious. She was also doing well academically.

Fast-forward to her senior year. Her team had not gotten off to a good start. The day before the sixth game of that year, I received a text from Jo saying that she was going to start in their next home game. It would be the first time she started in a college game. It was again a mid-week game, but there would be no doubt about what Cindy and I would do. We traveled to Abilene the next day, excited for Jo to begin a journey that would finally realize her potential.

Jo played a good game. She scored 10 points and played an all-around good game. Some of the parents in the stands even complimented Cindy and me on how well Jo was playing. Like us, they were looking forward to seeing how she could continue to help the team win moving forward. ACU was well ahead in the game and Coach Lavender sat Jo down midway through the second half to get some other players in the game. Cindy and I assumed that her night was over, but we were more than happy about that because it had been a successful game for Jo.

To our surprise though, with just about five minutes to play, Jo was inserted back in the game. Just a few minutes later, our world would be rocked again. Jo went up for a jump shot from the right corner and something again "popped" in that right knee. Many of the ACU fans knew of Jo's journey. At first, Cindy and I remained in the stands, not wanting to embarrass her by having her parents come out of the stands to check on her. But as she laid there in pain, not getting up, I knew I had to go to her. As I walked on the edge of the court to the far baseline where she laid, I thought to myself I could have heard a pin drop in this 4400-seat arena. Could this awful nightmare be happening again?

When I got to Jo, I remember her crying and looking at me, asking how could this be happening. I tried to console her, but frankly, I needed consoling myself. I put on a brave face and helped her, along with others, back to the training room. "How could this be God's plan for her?" was a thought that soon came to my mind. Cindy and I had believed that Jo had heard from God more than two years ago when she decided to come back after her second ACL surgery. How could this be the bitter end?

The trainers were nearly certain that she had torn her ACL again. I had to walk out of the training room and compose myself, as I was so overcome with emotion that I thought I was going to faint. There was a whirlwind of emotions in Jo, Cindy, and me, as well as her teammates and some of the other parents.

That night, I gathered some of her closest teammates and Coach Lavender in our hotel room, where Jo was going to spend the night with us. We were going to pray some believing prayers, believing that God would either confirm through an MRI that she didn't have a torn ACL, or if she did, that He would miraculously heal her. It just seemed right that one of those two things would happen in this situation.

Well, neither of those things happened. Jo's basketball career was officially over. The MRI the next day confirmed that her ACL had once again been torn. The exact words of the MRI report were "there is a paucity of reconstructed anterior cruciate fibers and a large amount of edema within the fibers." In other words, there was virtually nothing left of that second ACL replacement that had been completed two years earlier.

Since we did not want Jo to try to recover from another ACL surgery during the school year, we all agreed that that she would brace up her knee so she could get around campus and complete her senior year of school and have the ACL surgery at the end of her Spring semester, some six months later. However, since the MRI revealed other injuries to her knee beside the ACL, Jo did have microfracture surgery one month later in January to repair those specific injuries in her knee. During that surgery, the surgeon confirmed that the ACL was indeed torn, but did not repair the ACL. I should also mention that by this time Jo and Casey had been in a committed relationship since their sophomore year and that they had begun to discuss marriage.

Jo graduated from ACU that spring. It was now time to schedule the ACL portion of the surgery and we did so for May of that year. Since it had been six months since her injury, the surgeon wanted to get another MRI to ascertain the current state of her knee. During those six months, Cindy and I did a lot of praying together. We would often go up to our church, Woodlands Church, and pray outside at the cross in the middle of a large fountain the church has. We took great solace in it, as it was a peaceful place where we felt the presence of Christ with us in a special way.

Although our original prayer of seeing Jo realize her potential on the court was not going to be answered, we would still pray for a miracle healing of her ACL. However, we knew that we also had to pray for God's will to be done in the situation. That season of our lives was probably the best time of consistent prayer that Cindy and I have had together. We grew closer to the Lord and to each other.

We went in for Jo's pre-surgery appointment to discuss the results of the MRI, what she could expect from the surgery, and her projected recovery activities and timeframe. Once again, our world would be rocked, but this time in a good way! The MRI report had come back and this time the report said that her ACL was "INTACT"! It is easy to remember that word because we all stared at it for some time. The exact wording of the MRI report was "the graft (ACL) appears intact and demonstrates normal signal."

ACLs do not regenerate on their own. Once they are torn, they can only be repaired through replacement surgery. Yet, here we were looking at a report that said her ACL was *intact*. The doctor had no explanation for it. But we knew the explanation — God had chosen to be gracious to Jo and our family and heal her knee.

To this day, some ten years later, she has not had another ACL surgery. There is a simple explanation for that — surgery was not necessary! In order to remember the moment, remind her of God's graciousness toward her, and to build her faith daily, Jo had the before and after MRI reports framed. The miracle that Jo experienced remains the only physical miracle that anyone in my family has experienced.

As I think back on this story, I am reminded of two moments of big faith that made all the difference. The first was Jo's decision to return and play right before her sophomore year; a decision motivated by what she was convinced God was calling her to do. Reflecting on this now, that decision did not make a lot of sense from a strictly human perspective. She had experienced two torn ACLs, had been through two surgeries, and was likely not going to ever regain her athleticism and talent.

Besides, what did it matter in the long-run whether she had a good college athletic career? Her overall health should have been of paramount importance, over-riding her desire to continue playing. Yet, we know now that the decision was a prompting of the Holy Spirit.

The second was the on-going decision for Cindy and me to continue to pray for healing. Keep in mind, neither of us had ever experienced such a dramatic physical healing. Yet, we believed it was possible because we believed God's Word. A word of caution here. I really do not think our prayers "caused" God to be gracious toward our family. However, I do know Jesus Christ chose to intervene, and as a result, our faith was made stronger. That was certainly at least part of His purpose for the situation.

What really happened as a result of Jo, Cindy, and me believing God for big things? Obviously, we all got to experience a real miracle; a real intervention of Jesus Christ in our lives. It is absolutely awesome to know and reflect on that. But I think more importantly, as a result of Jo's situation, we had the opportunity to earnestly seek Christ for a prolonged period (three years).

Even if God had chosen not to heal Jo, each of our relationships with Christ had grown. When it is all said and done, there is nothing more important in a person's life than growing in intimacy with Christ. Often, that growth does not take place without adversity. The healing was the icing on the cake, but when I reflect on it, it was not the most important thing. It was the growth in intimacy with Christ that mattered much more because that will last into eternity.

We also have a real testimony of God's faithfulness to tell and encourage others in that. Hopefully, this chapter is doing just that for you. And don't forget, without Jo following Christ to come back for her sophomore year, she and Casey would not be married today, and we would not have two precious gifts from God — Trace and Trent, two of our five grandchildren.

I want to emphasize an important point here. Note how God did not answer our prayers exactly how we had planned. In our view, Jo would have been healed (or not injured to begin with), had her athleticism and skill immediately restored, and would have completed a nice college basketball career. But how would that have compared to what God chose to do instead?

He had a plan all along. Not exactly our plan, but a much better plan. As the keynote verse of this chapter says in Matthew 7:9-11, God will give us exactly the gifts that we need and better than we could imagine. I can give testimony that this verse could not be more true.

So, what did our family learn from this, and what can you possibly learn as well? I learned that "Big Faith" should be a characteristic of every Christian. Many Christians today tend to have a more "practical faith," assuming that God does not often intervene in miraculous ways. Nothing could be further from the truth. I suggest you read Lee Strobel's book, *The Case for Miracles*. You will discover that the miraculous activity of God is on-going still today.

I also learned that God desires us to have the type of faith that simply trusts Him and leaves the results up to Him. Jesus said in Matthew 17:20 that, ***"If you have faith as small as a mustard seed, you can say to this***

mountain, move from here to there and it will move. Nothing will be impossible for you." A mustard seed is a very small seed. We just need to start with simple faith and God can take it from there.

The answer may not always be as expected, but it will always be exactly what God planned all along. Which, by definition, is better than anything we can imagine.

Finally, I learned that big faith is critical to the spiritual development of each of us. Big faith can take us through journeys in life that we otherwise would not have experienced; journeys that can accelerate our growth in Christ. We should not have blind faith though. We should prayerfully consider what God is leading us to believe and look hard at God's Word for direction. When we do, the Holy Spirit will reveal what we are to pray about and work toward.

One other thought before closing. Big faith is not a one-time event. Rather, it should be an on-going activity in the believer's life. Sure, there may be times when an extra measure of faith is needed. Big life events can really define the depth of our faith. But each day will likely require faith even in the small things.

Some Christians have the spiritual gift of faith as described in 1 Corinthians 12:9, with the ability to believe big things and encourage others to do so as well. But if that is not a gift God has blessed you with, you can still exercise uncommon faith every day. It is an expectant, hopeful way to live.

When the time comes, do not be afraid to step out in faith in ways that you may not be comfortable with. It could turn into a major blessing as it did for my family. Stay consistent in God's Word and prayer, and I am sure God will present you with opportunities to exercise your faith in extraordinary ways.

CHAPTER 19

Finishing Strong

I have fought the good fight,
I have finished the race,
I have kept the faith.
Now there is in store for me the crown of righteousness,
which the Lord, the righteous Judge,
will award to me on that day — and not only to me,
but also to all who have longed for His appearing.
2 Timothy 4:7-8

Everyone loves a good "finisher" in sports. You know, the person who performs in the clutch at the end of a game. The player who wants the ball in their hands because they are confident they will perform with the game on the line, or the quarterback who brings his team from behind in the fourth quarter to win the game. I recently looked up which quarterback had the most fourth quarter come from behind wins in NFL history. Not surprisingly, it was Peyton Manning with 43 such wins in the final quarter. That is more than two-and-a-half seasons of wins! Ben Roethlisberger, with my beloved Pittsburgh Steelers, is tied for sixth with John Elway, each having 31, or nearly two full seasons, of come from behind victories.

All sports fans would say that they love a come-from-behind winner. Or put another way, they love a player who can "finish" even when the odds are against him or her. Men or women athletes who are good finishers are the most respected people in their sports.

So, how do we translate this "finishing" idea to the game of life? In the keynote passage of this chapter, Paul is reflecting on his life. Feeling certain that he is at the end of his life, he is commenting on how he has "left it all on the field" as we like to say in sports. Paul had given it his all — he had fought the good fight, finished the race, and kept the faith.

Don't we all want to be able to declare what Paul did in this passage? As I write this chapter, I am 62 years old. According to life expectancy charts, I am in the last quarter of my life. It is the fourth quarter for me. I have observed in the last few years that I have begun to think a lot more about this "finishing strong" concept. It may well be one of the primary motivators for me to write this book. And while there is nothing wrong with me reflecting more on my life now and how I want to finish my life, I am also of the mindset that I should have started this thought process long ago.

You may be reading this book as a 10-year-old, or a 100-year-old, or somewhere in between. I would propose to you that every single one of us who are believers in Christ should be thinking about finishing strong, regardless of our age. James 4:13-14 reminds us of this concept when it says, *"Now listen, you who say, 'Today or tomorrow we will go to this city or that city, spend a year there, carry on business and make money.' Why, you do not even know what will happen tomorrow."*

In addition to this passage, we are reminded in other places in the Bible that we do not know if we will be given another day. With this in mind, shouldn't every single one of us be thinking about finishing strong, regardless of our age? Shouldn't there be a sense of urgency at any age about the way we finish this life? Sure, it is admittedly easier to focus on it when we are older, but that does not mean every person should not focus on it right now.

So, if I have convinced you that you ought to be thinking about finishing strong in life, just as the apostle Paul described, let's think about what this would look like. Although it might sound a bit morbid to some, I would assert that we ought to start by thinking about how we want to feel about our relationship with Christ when we take our last breath. I think most of us would agree that we will want to be in the strongest relationship with Him that we have ever been. We will want to be closer to Him on that day than we were just the day before.

So many of us are concerned about making the right decisions in life — decisions about marriage, where to work, money, where to live, just to name a few. Those are all important things that we should be seeking guidance from the Lord in prayer. But those decisions will come more naturally and with less angst if our priority is to simply "follow Jesus." Kerry Shook, Pastor of Woodlands Church where I attend, once said in a sermon, "Follow Jesus, and the right path will find you."

In other words, instead of focusing on the outcome (related to marriage, job, etc.), focus on following Christ. Said another way, make your priority pursuing an intimate relationship with Jesus Christ and watch how all of your life decisions begin to become clearer.

All the great people of the Bible made it a point to obey and follow and then trust God for the results. I made that point in the *Obedience vs. Passion* chapter related to Joseph, the earthly father of Jesus. Joseph simply did what God told him to do, even though he did not know the outcome of the journey he was about to embark on. Abraham did the same thing, and so did David, Daniel, and Paul, to name a few.

At Paul's conversion on the road to Damascus, Paul hears the voice of Jesus, falls to the ground, and is temporarily blinded. Jesus tells him simply in Acts 9:6, ***"Now get up and go into the city, and you will be told what you must do."*** Right then and there, Paul began the process of "finishing strong," which starts with obeying and following Jesus. From the moment of his conversion, he set out on the adventure of following Jesus, no matter the cost.

So, how do you finish strong? You start right where you are today, no matter your age, or the depth of your relationship with Christ, and you simply start to follow Jesus. You set out on a journey of getting to know him better today than you did yesterday. You begin to say "yes" to Jesus even before He reveals specific plans to you for your life. Your mindset is one of "yes," not one of "let me first evaluate all the facts" before I say yes to what Christ has for me. If you sincerely think about it, finishing strong can be defined as saying yes to Jesus in every challenge He brings your way. As Colossians 3:2 says, our mind is set on *"things above, not on earthly things."*

Granted, the stage of your life may dictate the level at which you can pursue ministry outside the workplace. For me, having left the corporate world five years ago, I have the time to pursue things that God has laid on my heart that I would define as activities in pursuit of finishing strong — like meeting with a number of men in one-on-one discipleship and evangelistic relationships, leading a Home Group at our church, volunteering at the local Crisis Pregnancy Center, and being on the Board of a Christian University (Waynesburg University in Waynesburg, PA.). But those activities are just the results of my attempt to follow Jesus. My attempt to follow Jesus is what caused those things to happen. I opted to say yes to the opportunities Christ presented to me.

Finishing strong, however, is not just about engaging in ministry outside the workplace. In the chapter on *Making Your Work Spiritually Significant*, I discuss the idea of creating margin right where you are in the workplace. I encourage you to re-read that chapter to incorporate what you do in the workplace into finishing strong. In addition, the chapter on *Producing Spiritual Fruit* speaks to how we can have the attitude and take the necessary actions to finish strong. In reality, every single one of the chapters in this book contains an aspect of finishing strong. Anything that draws us into a closer relationship with Christ will necessarily cause us to finish stronger in Christ.

Paul gives us further insight into what makes "strong finishers," in 2 Timothy 4:8 when he says that those who finish strong can be defined as *"all who have longed for His appearing."* In other words, you cannot finish strong unless you have deeply sought Him out — unless you have "longed for His appearing" in your life.

That is the way Paul describes his fellow strong finishers in this passage. So, if you want to finish strong in life, do not wait another day. Begin to long for Jesus in your life; begin to follow Him and begin to say "yes" to Him.

Do not wait for tomorrow to be counted by Jesus to be among the strong finishers in life. After all, Jesus was the ultimate Finisher. God sent Him to fulfill a specific earthly ministry that brought glory to God and then to lay down His life as a sacrifice for our sins. In Jesus's "finishing" prayer just before His crucifixion, He tells God, *"I have brought you glory on earth by finishing the work you gave me to do"* (John 17:4).

The author of Hebrews defined Jesus as *"the author and finisher of our faith"* (Hebrews 12:2 NKJV). No one ever regretted finishing strong in life. I promise you that you will not regret it either. Every hardship that you may endure as a Christ-follower will have been all worth it in the end when He says to you, *"well done good and faithful servant"* (Matthew 25:23).

Finally, for those of you like me in the Fourth Quarter of Life, I want to encourage you to have an even greater sense of urgency about the way you will finish life. I have made the point in this chapter that everyone should be thinking about finishing strong, regardless of age. But it does not take a brain surgeon to know that those of us in the fourth quarter have a greater chance, statistically, of "finishing" sooner in this life.

Do not wait another day to get started on finishing. Improve your intimacy with Christ every day through God's Word and prayer, seek out strong relationships with other believers for support and encouragement, be ready to share Christ with non-believers, be faithful to disciple those whom God has led you to, be ready to say "yes" to whatever God leads you to, and take spiritual risks that would be honoring to Christ.

Like I desperately want to do myself, I encourage you to "leave it all on the field" before you leave this earth. And hopefully, this book has given you some new perspectives to consider in the on-going challenge to finish strong. Thank you for joining me on this journey.

Keynote Scripture Verses

The keynote Scripture citations at the start of each chapter are shared here for your easy reference.

1) My Personal Spiritual Journey.
     Crossing the Line of Faith.   John 5:24

2) Living a Life of Purpose   2 Corinthians 5:5

3) Making the Most of Every Opportunity   Ephesians 5:15-16

4) Making Your Work Spiritually Significant   Colossians 3:17

5) Producing Spiritual Fruit   Matthew 28:18-20

6) Loving Others Not Like You   Ephesians 4:31-32

7) Disciple-Making   2 Timothy 2:2

8) Becoming a Patriarch or Matriarch   James 3:13

9) Trusting Christ in Uncertain Times   Colossians 3:2

10) Humility   Matthew 5:3

11) Grumbling, Gratitude, and Unwholesome
    Talk   Philippians 2:14

12) Don't Worry   Matthew 6:27

13) Forgiveness   Matthew 5:23-24

14) Spiritual Disciplines   John 15:5

15) Giving   2 Corinthians 9:7

16) Unity Among Believers   John 17:23

17) Obedience vs. Passion   Philippians 2:5-8

18) Big Faith   Matthew 7:9-11

19) Finishing Strong   2 Timothy 4:7-8

ACKNOWLEDGMENTS

Thank you to all the friends and family members who helped edit the manuscript and encouraged me to complete this book.

A special thanks to Mark Paling, my friend and brother in Christ, who tirelessly edited the manuscript and took a special interest in the writing of this book.

I am also grateful to Steven Howard, my publishing coach, who provided guidance, direction, and encouragement during the editing and publishing process.

ABOUT THE AUTHOR

Mark Harner is a resident of Spring, TX, just north of the Houston metropolitan area. He has been married to his wife, Cindy, for 39 years and they have four grown children (Josh, Jenna, Jaymie, Joanna) and five grandchildren (Levi, Trace, Hayden, Trenton, and Mayleigh).

Mark completed his corporate career in 2014, leaving Waste Management in Houston after 14 years as a financial Vice President. Prior to Waste Management, Mark was the Chief Operating Officer for an outsourcing division of Price Waterhouse Coopers in Atlanta, GA. Before that, he held various financial management positions with Tenneco in both Newport News, VA and in Houston. He began his career with Deloitte in Pittsburgh, PA after graduating from Waynesburg University (PA) in 1979. Mark passed the CPA exam in 1980 and gained his MBA in 1990 from Old Dominion University in Norfolk, VA.

Upon leaving Waste Management, Mark obtained his Texas real estate license and represents clients in both commercial and residential real estate, as well as personally investing in both residential and commercial real estate. He obtained his real estate broker's license in 2019.

Mark is a past Board Chair of Waynesburg University (2014-2017) in Waynesburg, PA, his alma mater, and continues in his service on the Board, which began in 2010.

He is a member of Woodlands Church in The Woodlands, TX and has held various lay leadership roles there. He also volunteers at the local Crisis Pregnancy Center, counseling the young men who come into the Center with their wives or girlfriends. Additionally, Mark spends a good deal of his time in one-on-one evangelism and discipleship relationships with men. In his spare time he enjoys golf.

Made in the USA
Monee, IL
06 September 2019